BIG DUMB EYES

NATE BARGATZE
BIG DUMB EYES

Stories from a Simpler mind

GRAND
CENTRAL

New York Boston

Grand Central Publishing
Hachette Book Group
1290 Avenue of the Americas, New York, NY 10104
grandcentralpublishing.com
@grandcentralpub

First Edition: May 2025

Grand Central Publishing is a division of Hachette Book Group, Inc. The Grand
Central Publishing name and logo is a registered trademark of Hachette Book
Group, Inc.

The publisher is not responsible for websites (or their content) that are not owned
by the publisher.

The Hachette Speakers Bureau provides a wide range of authors for speaking
events. To find out more, go to hachettespeakersbureau.com or email
HachetteSpeakers@hbgusa.com.

Grand Central Publishing books may be purchased in bulk for business,
educational, or promotional use. For information, please contact your local
bookseller or the Hachette Book Group Special Markets Department at
special.markets@hbgusa.com.

Library of Congress Control Number: 2024952822

ISBNs: 978-1-5387-6846-4 (hardcover), 978-1-5387-6848-8 (ebook),
978-1-5387-7491-5 (signed edition), 978-1-5387-7490-8 (B&N signed edition)

Printed in the United States of America

LSC-H

Printing 1, 2025

For Laura and Harper, who always tell me
to be funny before every show.

CONTENTS

BIG DUMB EYES

INTRODUCTION:
THE MOST WORDS

I was on a call with the publisher, and they asked me what I wanted to call my book. So I'm like, "Okay. I got the perfect title. *Big Dumb Eyes.*"

And there was this silence on the other end.

Finally they go, "Uh, that is really not the kind of book we had in mind here. That sounds way too dark. Um. Kind of inappropriate, actually."

So I try to explain, right? I'm like, "Well, the thing is, whenever people talk to me, they always speak real slow. They pause after each word, like I'm not all there. Like I can't follow. And it's all because I got these big dumb eyes."

Then they go, "Ohhhhhh! Right. Okay. You talk kinda funny with that Southern accent. We thought you said 'Big *Demise.*'"

From then on, they would only communicate with me over email. By the way, what does "demise" mean anyway? Wait, I'm gonna look it up.

Ohhhhhh. De-*mise*. This book is definitely not that.

You might be a little nervous opening these pages, because I am very on the record about not liking to read books. It's a big part of my act, going on about how every book is just the most words. How it never lets up, and there's just more and more words until it's like, "What are you talking about? Please, just make it stop."

And here I am, writing one of my own.

But you're in for a real good time. Real good. Because I have taken everything bad about books and made it the best. So I can personally guarantee that you will love this book. Or at least that it is, in fact, a book. Because that is what I've been told.

Now, is it perfect? Let's not get crazy. I mean, it has a lot of pages. And I wanted lots more pictures. But it's pretty darn close, because this is the very first book in the history of the world that was written to not be a whole complicated thing. I'm not saying I wrote it for cats and dogs, but I bet they could knock a couple chapters out if they put their minds to it.

It's light. It's funny. It's relaxing. It's full of a bunch of stories about me and my hometown in Tennessee, my friends and my family, my old car named Old Blue, and how I flunked bowling my only semester in college. There's another chapter about how I was almost a genius, but I swear that is not a contradiction. So, basically I talk about the same kind of stuff I talk about on stage, but with new stories that have more fun details and background on everything and everyone in what I like to call Nateland.

This book is never trying to say anything even close to important. At first, I had a thirty-page chapter right in the middle called "The Meaning of Life," and I really do think I had it all figured out, but we got to the last draft of the book, right before publication, and I was like, "No! Too important! *Delete*." And now I forgot it.

You can read this book anywhere or any way you want. You can read it in bed. You can read it upside down. You can read it in the car, but only when you're driving. That's a joke, in case that is not clear. When you're done, you can leave it on your coffee table. I tried to tell the publisher to make it an actual coffee table, like Kramer's book in *Seinfeld*, but they said I'd need to write a lot more words for a book that big, so that was out.

You can read this book from beginning to end, or you can open it to any random chapter you want and you'll be just fine. There isn't any real order. No rhyme or reason behind much of anything. I was trying to think of one big chapter that said everything I ever wanted to say about food, then I realized my one big idea was "I love food. I love to eat food. Food is good." So instead I have a few smaller chapters about me and food I'm thinking of calling "Bites." Or maybe "Snacks." Or probably "Random Food Things." Either way, you won't need any special information to read any of it. You won't need facts or opinions or, like, smarts. I promise, you won't find that pesky stuff here. So just dive right in.

As I was learning to read, one of the most annoying things about books was having to keep track of all the characters' names. It's possible I shouldn't have started with *War and Peace*. So in my book, I will always remind you who I'm talking about, even if you met them before. Like my friend P-P comes up in a few chapters, and I will always helpfully remind you that he's called P-P because he got hit in the pee-pee by a football when he was in high school. Also because I love reminding P-P of that same story. How you doin', P?*

I will make sure to have some breaks, a few blank pages to help you keep your head above water, just in case you're crazy enough to read the book from front to back, which I don't even know if that's allowed. And I promise you there will not be lots of big words, because—I'm sorry, "'cause"—I don't like them.

There is one thing I should clear up, and that has to do with how I talk. Actually, the publishers told me I had to add this note, I think because they still feel burned by the whole "demise" thing.

---

*We've always written his name as "P," or if you wanna get formal, "P-P." Some might argue we should spell it out, but I've never been good with biological terms.

1. When I write "golly," it should actually be read as "*gaaaaaaaahhhhhhly!*"
2. Take any word that you say, and I probably say it different. Like "boil" is really "bowl." Though come to think of it, I don't think "boil" is actually in the book. But I do bowl. Whatever. Just read it in my voice and you'll have way more fun.
3. If you haven't actually heard my voice before, I talk slow. It doesn't feel slow to me. But you are not me. And I am not you.

And that's all you need to know. If you forget, just come right back to the beginning, and it'll be right here waiting for you.

Proof that I let my daughter Harper write this book for me.

THE BIGGEST LITTLE SPEED TRAP IN TENNESSEE

I grew up in this tiny little town in Tennessee that thought it needed six police officers. I'd say no one knew why we had so many police officers, except we did know why. They were there to give us all speeding tickets.

That was it. That was the only reason.

They weren't there to fight crime or stop bad guys from doing bad things. I'm sure there was some of that. But even if we wanted to do something bad to someone, we kinda couldn't, because we pretty much all knew each other. If somebody broke the law, it would be like, "Okay, let's talk about this at the church barbecue with the other twelve people in our town, half of whom are apparently cops."

My town was so tiny it actually existed *inside* another tiny town. Seriously. You can look at a map of Tennessee and you'll find a little blob called Old Hickory, and inside that little blob you'll find an even smaller, blobbier blob called Lakewood, which is so small and so blobby I usually only talk about Old Hickory in my act. I do not know how it is legally possible for one town to exist inside another town—and I never will, because that would require me to read a book—but it must be legal, because Lakewood existed, and it was my home.*

My parents had moved us there in the early nineties—my mom says 1991 or 1992 or maybe 1993, and she's the one in the family who's good with dates. So I was twelve years old. Or thirteen. Or fourteen. Or fifteen or eleven depending on the month, which she says was definitely December or absolutely July. Whatever it was, it was a good year. And extremely memorable.

Our previous town was, in fact, Old Hickory, which was one or two miles down the road. So yeah. It was a big transition for all of us.

Lakewood is the kind of place where if you go to the school and look at old class photos, you'll see pictures of your buddies' grandparents when they were kids, because no one ever leaves. It's the kind of place where if you fall down a cliff and get a concussion, your neighbor will pick you up and carry you back to your mom. I know this because it happened to me. It's the kind of place where there are two different families both named Thompson, then they had kids, and two of those kids got married. Now I can't figure out if that means there's one Thompson family or three.

In the winter, if there was a half inch of snow, people would just go crazy. We barely ever saw any snow in the South, we had no idea what was going on. Everything would shut down. We're talking schools, offices, grocery stores, hospitals, everything. Like you'd have emergency surgeries scheduled, patients flatlining on the edge of death, and the doctor would call in and go, "You kidding me? Have you seen those roads? I'm going sledding!"

And that's what we'd do. The entire town would gather at the one big hill that was behind our church and right next to the golf course.

---

*I say "existed" because at some point they decided to make it unincorporated, which is a technical term my mom told me. So it kinda isn't there anymore, even though we all still call it Lakewood. Anyway, talk to my mom.

Everyone would be there. Friends, neighbors, all three Thompson families—or two or one, or whatever—we'd all go. We'd take trays and trash can lids and we'd flop down on our bellies, me on the bottom, my sister on top, my brother sandwiched in between, and we'd bolt right down that single snowy hill, and after five minutes it was nothing but mud. Just pure slop. We'd keep going and going till we were totally covered in muck. Like, "Woohoo! It's a winter wonderland!"

My dad got so excited one year he went out and bought one of those classic red sleds with the metal runners like something out of *A Christmas Story*. Got to the mud hill and it was like trying to slice through a Big Mac with a butter knife. I mean, slicing through a Big Mac with a butter knife would be insane to do. I feel dumb even writing it, because no one would ever try that. I don't think a butter knife has ever even been *near* a Big Mac. But if you did try to cut one, and you used a butter knife, it would be as effective as going down that muddy hill on my dad's sled. That's all I know, and that is the kind of town I'm from.

It was also the kind of town that didn't need any police officers, except for one reason, and that was to give people speeding tickets.

That was all the Lakewood PD did. The six of them would get to work in the morning and they'd look at each other and go, "What's it gonna be today? Drug busts?"

"Nope."

"Murder?"

"Uh-uh."

"Grand theft auto?"

"Nah."

"How about we park across from the Piggly Wiggly and catch anyone going 35 in a 30?"

"Sounds right to me."

Everyone knew the speed trap was there, but we all kept speeding anyway. I don't know why. There was just something about Old Hickory Boulevard that made you want to speed on it. I mean, it's four lanes, with a lane in the middle. So is that five lanes? Whatever it is, you ain't going the speed limit. But honestly, the whole thing was so ridiculous it was kind of fun.

One time they got us while we were driving to church on a Sunday morning. My dad was behind the wheel, drinking a Big Red. Big Red is a cream soda. It's red and it's delicious. It's also why my dad has diabetes. He loved it so much he would go down to Kentucky on weekends and buy cases of the stuff, because that was the only place you could get it in old-fashioned glass bottles, and everyone knows soda always tastes better in bottles than cans.

This policeman pulled us over, looked at my dad and us kids all dressed up to go to church at 9 a.m., and he thought, "These people are up to no good." So he spots the fizzy red beverage my dad's drinking, and he goes, "What you got in there? Is that alcohol?"

My dad goes, "No, Officer, it's a cream soda. It's red and it's delicious."

The cop thinks about this for a second. "Well, I should prolly get a little sip. Just to be sure."

He took that sip. And just like that he also got diabetes.

Once, the Lakewood PD tried to pull over my mom, and she actually managed to lose them in the neighborhood. I'm serious. This is a thing that really happened.

My mom heard the sirens, she saw the flashing lights, she said, "Nope, not today, Po-Po," and she outran this cop behind the wheel of a used Mazda.* She probably had to floor it just to get up to 35, that's how fast that car was. And this neighborhood is like ten blocks long. You couldn't lose your wallet on one of these streets. I have physically gone to this spot, put on a blindfold, turned myself around, and tried

---

*For people who keep track of these things, this was not my old Mazda "Old Blue," which we discuss in another chapter, but a different old Mazda that was red. If my mom ever called it anything, it was basically just "My Old Mazda" or "That Car." She never was much for car nicknames.

to get confused, and I could not do it. But my mom in her Mazda was able to lose this cop.

To be clear, she's usually a law-abiding citizen, but she didn't want to have to tell my dad she got us another ticket so soon after we got busted for driving under the influence of soda pop.

Eventually, me and my brother grew up and moved out, and my parents and my little sister moved to a different town, Mount Juliet, about ten miles away. It wasn't that big, nothing in Tennessee really is, but it was still about twice the size of Lakewood. It wasn't as blobby. It had more than just one muddy hill in the winter. Its police did real police things.

And eventually, Lakewood lost its police department. I don't mean there was a budget cut or a downsize. Once the town became unincorporated, the cops disappeared. One second the Lakewood PD was sitting across from the Piggly Wiggly, shaking down families on their way to church, and the next second they were gone. Just like that.

It was all right, I guess. But still, we were kind of sad. They were *our* pointless, annoying cops, and now they were gone. Like maybe we should've made special trips back to the speed trap. Driven even *faster*. *More* dangerous. Just to give them more to do, even if it was the only thing they ever did.

To this day, whenever I'm driving through on my way to visit family, heading down that single main street where no one ever breaks a single law, I always put my foot on the brake and make sure I'm going under 30, in memory of the Lakewood Police Department.

Then, to be honest, I do speed up. Because the street has too many lanes to go that slow.

RAISED BY A CLOWN

Back when I was a little kid, my dad was a clown. I don't mean that as an insult or something. I mean he was an actual, real-life professional clown.

And let me tell you, having a clown for a dad was not easy.

Not because he wasn't a good dad, because he was, but because he was an even better clown. And how was I supposed to compete with that? Maybe if he had been one of those weird, spooky clowns that everyone always says they're afraid of. But there is nothing scary or spooky about a clown named Yo-Yo who wears a bright yellow wig and does magic tricks.

For my seventh birthday, we had a little party at the park. All my friends came. It was the perfect day, the weather was nice, and my dad put on a magic show—and that's all my friends wanted to do. Just watch the show. They forgot that I, the birthday boy, the whole reason for this entire occasion, even existed. I walked a few feet over to the playground and called, "Hey guys, anyone want to swing with me?"

Everyone was like, "NO! Absolutely not!"

Not easy.

"All right, how about the sandbox? That sand is looking real nice today. Very clean. Lots of fine, clean sand grains. I bet we could make a castle. That would be neat."

"Um, are you still talking? We are literally watching a magic show by a clown named Yo-Yo. Stop making this day about you."

My dad was great at magic, but I had seen all the tricks before. The only reason he was hired for my party was because it's the only entertainment my parents could afford. So I sat there and swung by myself. If someone walking by saw the park from a distance, it looked like this little boy was just not being invited to this magic show.

All my friends' dads were normal dads who read the newspaper and worked at an office and did not walk around in bright orange tuxedos with big blue floppy shoes. My friends all lived in normal houses, where you walked in and saw normal-house things, like a rug and maybe a cat.

You walked into my home, and the first thing you'd see was a bag of thirty lemons, one stack of fake quarters, twenty lengths of rope, and about seven hundred million decks of cards. In fact, the people who now own our old house recently pulled up the carpet and literally found a dozen marked cards buried underneath. How do I know this? Last Halloween, my now-grown-up brother and sister went to our old house trick-or-treating with their kids, and up on the wall they saw this totally random framed picture of some of my dad's old cards. My brother and sister were like, "Why are our dad's old cards up on the wall?" The people who lived there were like, "Why were your dad's old cards under our floor?" Some questions are better left unanswered.

In high school, I got my first girlfriend. It was the kind of thing where you say you're "going out" even though you never actually go anywhere except maybe school and church. So, true love. But guess what? She wouldn't come to my birthday that year.

My dad, after all this time, was still performing at my birthdays. I mean, *you* try to top having a world-class magician at *your* birthday, okay? But later on I found out she was afraid my dad would do something silly in his act, like call her up to demonstrate a trick. I couldn't believe it. After all this time, I had finally found someone who thought my dad was a scary clown. She really was the love of my life.

Anyway, that ended the relationship. But as I look back on it now, fair enough. That is a lot to take in as a ninth grade girl.

My dad's story is like the stories of a lot of funny people I know, in that it doesn't start out funny at all.

This, by the way, does not include me. My childhood was pure dumb funny, but that pretty much only happened because my dad got all the miserable stuff out of the way.

First off, he's from Kentucky, which is obviously very bad, because it's not Tennessee. His mom was very good at bowling—she's actually in the Kentucky Bowling Hall of Fame—but she wasn't very good at being a mom. When my dad was about three, she left him outside the bowling alley because she didn't want to watch him while she played, and that's when he got bit in the face by a bulldog.

To this day, my dad still talks with a little bit of a speech impediment because of it. The bulldog tore from his cheek down to his chin and took part of his tongue. He had to have six and a half years of reconstructive plastic surgery, the kind where they take skin from other parts of your body and rebuild your face. So my dad likes to tell people that most of his face is actually his butt. It looks good—he just has real bad breath.

And yeah, he usually cracks that joke *right* when he meets someone. I mean, how am I supposed to compete with a dad that cool? How?

My dad's mom was basically what these days they'd call abusive. She and his dad were both alcoholics. Because of his speech impediment, my dad was placed in special ed and told he was stupid for most of his life. His mom pretty much agreed. By the time he reached high school, he wasn't good at reading, and he could hardly write at all.

The one good thing that happened to my dad during this time was meeting the lady who would eventually become my mom. The two of them met when they were in the eighth grade, at a local teen club. My father never had the guts to ask somebody to dance, because he was afraid they'd say no. So when he saw my mom, he sent his friend over to ask if she liked him. My dad likes to say that they asked seventeen girls, and he finally got back one yes.

My mom, because she's pretty much a living saint, finds this adorable. She went home the night of the dance, woke up her mom, and said, "Mom, you won't believe this, but I just met this boy. And I know that someday he and I will get married. I don't know how, but I know it."

Which is almost as good as the story of how I met my wife Laura working at Applebee's.

Well, even with my mom in his life, my dad was still having a lot of trouble at home. Once he graduated high school, my grandma made it pretty clear she didn't want him around anymore. So he ran away from home and went to Tennessee. I'd like to tell you that as soon as he crossed that state line his whole life turned around, but that ain't what happened. He lived on the street for a few months, and he tried to take his own life once, which he'll tell you was the dumbest thing he ever did. He'd basically hit rock bottom when he moved in with his cousin Ronnie, who was an assistant coach on the Vanderbilt basketball team.

If you know anything about Vandy's history with sports, you know Ronnie had it about as bad as my dad did. That was a joke, but only kinda.

Living with Ronnie and his wife Melinda was what finally started to turn things around. I don't think my dad had ever experienced what it meant to have a family before, but with those two he finally had one. My dad had this old shoulder injury from a fight he'd had with his mom, this time when she pushed him down the steps. So my dad started wearing a big cast to help fix it, and he couldn't move his arm or get it wet. One day, Melinda comes by and she goes, "You stink—you need a bath." So my dad goes, "What can I do? I can hardly move."

"Well, get some swim trunks on," she said. She ran the bath, put him in there, and she helped him wash off. He was seventeen years old. No one had ever been kind to him like that before.

Ronnie and Melinda, they went to church, and they got my dad to go with them. God, he learned, offered the same kind of grace, the same kind of mercy. He'd love my dad no matter what. He'd be there for him unconditionally. From there on, everything changed.

That last part, by the way, was what people in the South call testimony. That's just between me and you. Normally I try to play down the whole Southern thing. So don't tell a soul.

To be fair to my dad, he did try his best to make me part of his act. This was possibly a worse idea than trying to live on the streets of Nashville.

Back when I was in kindergarten, he did a show for my whole school in our big auditorium. I, of course, was very ready to accept my fate as the son of the neatest dad in town. I knew the drill. He would get attention, I would get a great show. It was fine by me. But my dad was like, "Son, I'm gonna give you a shot. This'll be your big break. You get to help me with a trick."

Now, I'm gonna be honest with you. I could spend the next two and a half pages trying to describe this trick to you with all my amazing skills with, like, words, and you still wouldn't get it. You have to kinda see it in action. But all you really need to know is that there was a little dog that was running between a couple boxes, trying to get a forbidden sausage, and all I was supposed to do was scream real loud every time the dog got close to getting the sausage.

That's it. That's all I had to do. Just scream on cue. Just lose my mind. I mean, I was five years old, so I pretty much spent most of my time like this anyway. It is a natural state of being for a child that age.

Even then, even with something that basic, my dad wasn't leaving anything to chance. We actually practiced. My dad and I stood there at home, and he was like, "Nathan, scream!" So I screamed. Over and over and over. Looking back, it kinda makes me wonder just how stupid I seemed back then. In between rehearsals, was my mom walking up to my dad and whispering, "I don't know—should you remind him to breathe too? This all feels so advanced!"

But you know what? I got that screaming down. I had that thing mastered, dude. I was a pro.

Then I got on stage, right next to my dad, in front of my entire school. And I froze. Terrified. Couldn't make a sound. I honestly doubt I was breathing either, which probably didn't help with the whole being-stupid thing.

So the dog is running back and forth, going from one box and into the other, and my dad is looking at me, and I'm opening my mouth as wide as I can and saying absolutely nothing. And then the final reveal, when magically, incredibly, the dog *somehow* appears out of the wrong box and eats the forbidden sausage.

Which was when I finally decided to scream: "BUT DAD, THERE'S A SECOND DOG!"

You see. The deal was that there were two dogs. The audience could only see one. But behind my dad, I could see the whole trick and noticed there were two dogs. I guess you could say I was the first Masked Magician.

And if you don't get that reference, it's probably a good thing neither of us went into magic.

Getting saved by Jesus was the beginning of my dad's career in magic. A tale as old as time.

Back in grade school, he'd met a teacher who used magic to make my dad want to read. This teacher was a very good sleight-of-hand guy, and he kind of planted the seeds of the magician my dad could become. But it wasn't until he got his life together in Tennessee that my dad realized he could tap into something else to make him really stand out—comedy.

His jokes came from a place of darkness. He believed we needed to laugh at ourselves—and at each other—otherwise we'd probably cry. Like his speech impediment. At first he was kinda embarrassed to talk. But as Yo-Yo the clown, who cared? He had his clown voice, and people loved it. Then eventually he realized he could still be funny without the wig and the makeup, so he left the clown act behind and did a different kind of magic.

His favorite trick was what he called the Straitjacket of Death. He's a huge Andy Kaufman fan, and Kaufman was a genius at doing these ridiculous stunts. So my dad came up with his own Kaufman-style routine. He'd perform at these little clubs where he'd get into a straitjacket, and the trick was—he never got out. He'd just keep struggling and struggling, and the show's supposed to be over, but he's still on the stage, struggling. Eventually he added a bit where a volunteer from the crowd would actually start fighting with him, trying to pull this thing off him.

These strangers would tear his shirt, stick their foot in his back. Like he'd get into actual fights—he eventually had to have back surgery from this stunt. But the audience loved it. They'd be dying laughing. He toured all over the world. He likes to say this trick made a living for his family. He'd probably say it put me through college if I didn't flunk out after a semester.

As for my dad and my grandma, they didn't speak for years. Honestly, me and my brother and sister don't have a ton of memories of her. It's not like he talked bad about her. It wasn't like he was bitter or held a grudge. They just weren't in each other's lives.

But then a couple years ago my dad's mom got sick, and he went to see her. He'd tried to connect with her a couple times before, but there was always a barrier. So this time he just said he was sorry. He started crying, and he told her he was sorry for not being a better son. He was sorry for not trying harder to make her a part of his family, for not doing more to give her a relationship with his kids. He goes, "I just need you to forgive me."

And it melted her. For the first time in his life, he finally felt close to his mom. He said he'd see her in Heaven, and they'd have a long time to straighten everything out. She died the next day.

I finally figured out that the best approach to take with my dad was, "If you can't beat 'em, join 'em." Except in this case I made him join me.

So yeah. I guess pretty much the opposite of that first thing I said.

It was back in 2007 when I was just getting started in comedy. I was living in New York, and I had just done my very first TV appearance on the show *CMT Comedy Stage* for Country Music Television. Some folks at Belmont University back in Nashville saw me and wanted me to do a show on campus. They were like, "We'll pay you a thousand dollars." And I was like, "That is more money than I've ever seen in my life. I am officially a billionaire."

But they also wanted me to go on stage for an hour. Which was terrifying, because I had enough material for maybe thirty minutes.

So I called up my dad and asked him to open for me. I told him I needed him to do at least thirty minutes, and—this was the most important part—I told him he couldn't be *too* funny. Like, for once in his life, could he please hold back just a tiny bit. He could have all his magic and all that, but please just let me be the funniest guy that night. Please.

And I offered to pay him two hundred bucks for the gig. I mean, what was I gonna do? You have to pay your openers.

The night of the show came around, and of course he didn't hold back at all. He absolutely *killed*. Like everyone was literally crying laughing, just rolling in the aisles he was so funny. Me and Laura had just gotten married, and this was the first time her parents had ever seen me or my dad perform. They came by to say hi after the show, and they were very polite to me. But I could tell—they really just wanted to meet my dad. When he finally walked over, their jaws dropped and they go, "You were *amazing*."

Like, "Are you sure *you* don't want to marry Laura instead? Doesn't that seem like a better arrangement for all parties?" I think they figured worst case I could just open for my dad and support their daughter that way. To this day, my father-in-law still brings up that show. My in-laws will come over for the holidays, and Laura's dad kinda shakes my hand real quick, then pushes right by me to ask for a card trick. And then my dad starts hunting under the floorboards.

But that night wasn't all bad. Opening for me was the first time my dad ever got to really introduce me to an audience. He started saying how proud he was of me, how filled with gratitude he was that so many people had come to watch me perform. And I like to think that he wasn't just grateful for how far I'd come, but for how far he'd come too. Because who I am and what I've done wouldn't be possible without him.

Whatever it was, he got this catch in his throat, and he just started crying. I still have him open shows for me to this day, and he still starts crying every single time. The crowd always soaks it up, because it's so incredibly authentic. He shines brighter than anyone else on that stage.

Oh, and he never saw a dime of the $200 I promised for our very first show. He still reminds me of that every chance he gets.

I WAS ALMOST A GENIUS

I was almost a nuclear scientist.

It was gonna be that or maybe an electric engineer. Or a doctor that does brain stuff. Or maybe a math teacher who teaches the hardest math on earth. You know, any of those jobs that take a lot of smarts. That was gonna be me.

Now, I know what you're thinking. You're thinking, "Nate, you're a stand-up comic. You're a pretty dumb guy." You're right. I am dumb. Now.

But I wasn't always like this. I used to be a genius. And I know I was a genius because back in the seventh grade I won the school science fair. It's true. I really did. I went up against the best and brightest, and somehow the judges were like, "This kid. The one with the big dumb eyes. He is the best of the best and the brightest of the brightest."

Like, all right, dudes. Whatever you say. I'm a genius.

Let's be straight, though, because this wasn't just any science fair. My town was a company town, and that company was DuPont. It started like a hundred years ago with a plant to make gunpowder, then they started making chemicals and stuff. I'll be honest, I never really knew what they did. I didn't ask. I walked by this factory every day and never once said, "Hey, what happens there?" Or maybe I did and just forgot. I'll get to that in a second.

I went to DuPont Hadley Middle School. The building was shaped like Mickey Mouse's head. I never saw it from above but they told us that and the way we walked in circles, I figured it was true. So our fair was judged by scientists from DuPont, and the prizes were given out by the head guy from DuPont, who we think might have been named Gary, but my mom's not sure. If it's not Gary, then it's something else. Anyway, the winner of our science fair then got to go compete in the citywide competition, and if you won the city you got to go to the state fair. And if you won that one? Well, sky's the limit.

I'm pretty sure Elon Musk and all the AI people all won their state science fair. I think that is the only way to become whatever Elon Musk actually is. Space scientist or something.

So all the serious students in our school, they worked their very hardest for this thing for weeks. Building big models, creating complicated demonstrations, testing exciting new theories. You know, science stuff.

Me? I waited until the day before and stole one of my dad's magic tricks.

My dad, as I talked about in the last chapter, is a professional magician, so he had lots of fun stuff around to choose from. I decided to not go for the fake dollar bill or the vanishing puppy. I was in junior high. I pulled out the big guns. Magnets.

The magnet my dad had wasn't huge—it was small enough to fit in a deck of cards—but it was really strong. Like this thing could move around metal objects through a four-inch table. It could also do something no other magnet on the planet could do. It could move stuff that *wasn't* made of metal. Like a chicken bone. And a wooden match. And a penny. Which is impressive because it's not some dumb metal nickel.

So the idea was you could put one of these objects in the palm of your hand and use the secret hidden magnet to make it look like you could move a chicken bone or a match with nothing but the power of your mine.

Now, you might point out that the chicken bone and matches and penny were all props that had slivers of iron in them. And if you did that, I'd imagine you would point out that it is "mind" and not "mine." So, you're not a very good time. But thankfully, I am a good time. Also, this was back in the 1900s so we all still believed in a little magic. The whole Mayan calendar debacle came pretty soon after. I was sink, line, and hooker on that one.

(About that last sentence, I do the *Nateland* podcast with Brian Bates, Aaron Weber, and Dusty Slay, and that's what I said instead of "hook, line, and sinker." I think I'm dyslexic. Which could be because of the . . . wait, I'll get to that. Don't let the horse get before the cart. Hey Bear!)

Back to the story. I looked at these things that were literally designed to make people doubt rational thought, and I said, "Science!" And I took that powerful secret magnet and that fake chicken bone into the school gym, and I stood right next to all the other kids with their serious experiments about dinosaurs and volcanoes, and I have no idea what exactly I said or did or why it was so special, but by the time I was done, those DuPont scientists were *blown away*!

Then all these science dudes ran back to their big fancy office, and they grabbed Gary and all the other science dudes, and they were like, "You would not believe it! Forget the cure for cancer! We got a kid who can make matchsticks move with the power of his brain! Granted, he doesn't look too bright, but still—we saw it with our own eyes! We're gonna be rich! We're gonna win the Nobel Prize! But first . . . first, let's give him first place in the school science fair." I never saw Gary again after that day.

None of that last paragraph is probably true, but it basically is. But I don't remember exactly.

The school had a big ceremony where they gave me a blue ribbon for first place. My parents, who were just as surprised as I was, tell me they were very proud on that great day and figured I'd spend the rest of my life doing, like, experiments or something.

For the citywide competition I was super excited. I really thought I had a chance to win this thing. Unfortunately, I will never know. Because we didn't even go. I think I had a baseball game, or someone had something, or maybe we were over science as a family. So we just dropped the magic trick off at the fair along with a short note on the bent posterboard backdrop that said, "Move the magnet below with the chicken bone."

We didn't win. But. If you go to Dupont Hadley, to this day my name should be on the wall in the office as winning the science award. They did tell me it would be there forever. I remember that because I thought it was so cool. I have not been up there to check, so if you're a student at Dupont Hadley and for some reason bought this book, please check it for me. You can let my parents know because they still live down the street.

Anyway, I know that all sounds pretty bad as far as me being a genius goes, but I didn't just win the science fair. I really was the smartest kid in seventh grade. At the end of the year, at the big school assembly, I won all the awards for smarts. I really did. History, math, and of course, science, with my amazing magnetic chicken bone.

They called my name so much I was uncomfortable. And then in the eighth grade they never called it, and I was also uncomfortable.

What exactly happened to my brain from the seventh grade to the eighth grade is the subject of a lot of heated debate in my family. And by "heated debate," I mean everyone agrees on the reason except me.

I'm 100 percent sure that over the summer break something got knocked loose in my head when I fell sixty-two feet off a cliff in our neighborhood and got a concussion. Me and my buddy Corey were hanging out, trying to climb down this cliff that overlooks Old Hickory Lake. We didn't have any rope or helmets or any safety equipment. I don't even know if they sold helmets back then.

But I slipped and fell. I hit my head on a rock on the way down, passed out, and went to the hospital in an ambulance. I think this had some kind of impact on my intelligence. My skull got, like, dented or something, and I was different after that. The accident left a mark on the back of my head that I still have to this day.

In case you don't believe me, my mom just helpfully sent me a picture of me from one of my specials with the mark circled, saying, "Here's that mark from when you hit your head."

It's in that circle, my mom says.

However smart I used to be in the seventh grade, you can see what my family thinks of me now. They also like to point out that there were stairs from the top of the cliff to the bottom literally *right next to where I was climbing*, so how bright could I have been before I fell?

According to my family, what really changed for me from the seventh grade to the eighth grade comes down to two words, and those two words are "Daniel Rucker."

The Rucker family moved to our town from Michigan right before I started eighth grade. The dad was a pastor, they had eight kids, and they all had red hair, although my mom says she is certain that only two of the Rucker children had red hair, and it is very important that we get this right. Redheaded or not, they were all really smart. Like, so smart. They didn't own a TV. They just read books. I had never seen anything like this before. Or if I had, I didn't remember, probably because of that dent in my brain.

The Ruckers were very nice. Maybe too nice. They were good at sports, they lived in a cool house behind the church, and I'm pretty sure my parents liked their kids better than they liked us. My brother and sister both had Ruckers in their grades, and my parents shrugged like, "Don't worry about studying. You got a Rucker. They'll wipe you out anyway."

My Rucker was Daniel Rucker, and my folks were just as encouraging. I told them there was a new kid in my class and he was my academic rival. My mom said, "I wish you'd play more with that Daniel Rucker boy. He's so nice and smart. I know *he'd* take the stairs at the cliff."

But I refused to back down. When eighth grade started, I worked so hard. I studied harder than I ever had studied. I did more math and science than ever before. And I read books. At least two.

All right, not really. The truth is, I barely even tried.

My brain was already broke to dumb from the fall. I probably never even read a page that year. And I was also starting to realize that for some reason I liked making people laugh more than I liked, you know, studying and stuff. That was good enough for me.

Somehow, though, I made it to the end of the eighth grade. I went to the final awards ceremony, and I watched as they called Daniel Rucker's name over and over again. I was sitting a few seats away, and I stared at those fancy certificates he had on his lap, all those prizes for good grades that used to be mine.

I stared at them so hard, focusing all my mind power, scrunching up my eyes, trying to get them to slowly move from his hands to my hands.

Nothing. And my dad's a magician.

RANDOM FOOD THING 1:
I GUESS SUSHI IS OLD

I found out recently that sushi is this, like, ancient food. This came as a huge surprise to me.

I said, "I don't know, but I'm pretty sure it was invented in 2008 in California."

And they're like, "No, it's from Japan, dude."

So I go, "All right, smart guy, then explain to me the origin of the California roll. Are you really telling me that some guy in prehistoric Japan somehow knew to name the most popular of all the rolls after some state in America? That was maybe or maybe not around? It makes no sense!"

I was actually talking to a sushi chef at an actual sushi restaurant at the time, so that felt pretty good, to know more than him. Like, checkmate, man. Then my wife Laura pointed out that the sign above the door said "Japanese Food." Which is just like Laura, to be a know-it-all who doesn't support local businesses.

Turns out that sushi has been around for two hundred years. So that's two hundred years of tradition and wisdom and fine-tuning all these ancient recipes, just so I could order it and go, "No cucumbers in the fried shrimp tempura, please."

But I gotta give the Japanese credit. That whole cream-cheese-on-the-Philadelphia-roll thing was genius.

MY SISTER THE ALIEN

Right around when she turned nine, my kid sister Abigail decided she was old enough to start buying people Christmas presents for the very first time.

It was 1997, and Abigail didn't have money, because really none of the Bargatzes had money back then, but there was a small change jar my parents kept right by the front door. My mom said Abby could use the nickels, dimes, and quarters for gifts, as long as she worked for it by separating and rolling all the change into those paper tubes that banks use. I guess because my sister was too young to send to the coal mines.

Abigail actually thought rolling the change was fun, because she was the kind of girl who thought that kind of stuff was fun. She was shy and quiet, with braces on her teeth and thick glasses. And if you think I have big eyes, this girl looked like Bambi just walked into a surprise party. Her best friend was a yellow parakeet she owned named Tweety Bird, which almost died once when it randomly flew into my dad's frying pan while he was cooking bratwurst. And another time when the dog almost ate it. And another time when it landed on a sticky pad for catching mice, and my dad had to shave off half of Tweety Bird's feathers to get it unstuck.

Her best friend was a parakeet.

So my sister had seen a lot for someone her age. She knew about life, she knew about death, she knew about birds flying into hot, crackling oil for no good reason. She liked doing her own thing, but she also wanted to be loved. Buying us gifts was a pretty big deal.

For most of the family, she stuck to the basics. I mean, this was a girl who named her yellow parakeet "Tweety Bird" after all. She went to Walmart and got my mom pajamas and my dad a tie, which was an interesting choice for a professional clown and magician who went to the office in a rainbow wig. For our brother Derek she got a video game for the PlayStation, which sounds impressive but was not. Instead of *Madden* or *NCAA Football*, it was some off-brand game no one had ever heard of, called *Ball* or something, about a sport that possibly didn't even exist. Just two random blobs passing a totally square "ball" back and forth over and over.

The game still had the clearance sticker on it—a bold statement coming from Walmart—and it broke the first time Derek played it. Though to be fair, that's because Abigail dropped my dad's bowling ball on top of the PlayStation because Derek refused to play *Ball* with her, breaking both the game *and* the PlayStation.

For me, though, my sister went all out. I was eighteen. I was her big brother. I might not have been the smartest guy in the world, or the strongest, or honestly good at anything at all—but to her none of that mattered. To her, I was the coolest guy ever. Sure, my car had a stick shift with a tennis ball knob, but I drove her *everywhere* in it. Yes, I got awful grades, but I was about to graduate *high school*. Probably! And okay, I never made the basketball team, but I was definitely a few inches taller than her. She had to look up to me! To Abigail, I could do no wrong. So she wanted to get me something cool. Something impressive.

And in 1997, nothing was cooler, nothing was more impressive, than the movie *Men in Black*. I mean, you had aliens, you had that funny dog, you had Will Smith in Ray-Bans, and, you know, Tommy Lee Jones, I guess. So yeah. Cool. Impressive. She got me a brand-new DVD of *Men in Black*. Also from Walmart. Maybe you can sense a theme here.

Abigail was so excited, she couldn't even wait for Christmas. She knew I was gonna love her present, and she wanted a taste of just how happy, just how *thrilled* her gift was gonna make me.

So the night before Christmas, when our presents were already wrapped and under the tree, she told our brother Derek to find out exactly how I'd react while she hid behind the corner and listened in. Derek was super subtle about it.

"Hey dude," he said, all smooth. "You like that movie *Men in Black*?"

And I went, "*Men in Black*? Are you kidding me? I *hate* that movie!"

She heard every word. And she was crushed. After all, what was she gonna do? Buy me a new gift? Christmas was tomorrow, and she'd already spent every last rolled penny from the change jar. She'd pinned all her hopes on her big brother absolutely loving these wacky CGI aliens, and I'd ruined everything.

Now, I want to make it clear that I had no idea my little sister was listening. I did not go out of my way to destroy her pug-in-sunglasses dreams. But the honest truth is, back then, maybe, just maybe, I would have. Because even though she was my sister, I was not always as nice to her as I should have been.

Though I was a lot nicer than Derek. Who really was the worst.

Abigail is about ten years younger than me, and seven years younger than Derek. So, a bit of an age gap. Maybe that's why she felt a little left out sometimes. Though to be fair, sometimes she did literally get left behind.

Like this one time when me, my dad, and my brother took Abigail with us to church, while our mom stayed home sick. Abby was four, and it was a Wednesday night, because we are Southern Christians so why not. Then when we got home, we realized my sister wasn't with us. Honestly, I don't even know what else to say about that. She just wasn't there.

This wasn't some crazy *Home Alone* thing where there were twenty of us rushing around trying to make a last-minute plane to Europe and Macaulay Culkin slept in and got bitter and weird. This was just us three dudes—me, my dad, and my brother—having ourselves a nice leisurely time, hanging out and talking to friends after church, driving home at a nice, relaxed pace, walking through the front door, and going, "Oh." Like, "Something seems off here. Can't quite put a finger on it. But . . . are we missing a human being?"

The first thing my dad does is go, "Do not tell your mother."

Next thing my dad does is put me and my brother in the car so we can head back to church at a slightly faster pace. Of course, if this had happened recently we would've had cell phones, so we could've just called or texted or sent out one of those loud alerts that freaks everyone out. So really, blame technology.

We get there, and this couple we know has my sister huddled in their car. They said, "We found Abigail wandering alone in the old church cemetery." Basically just passing from tombstone to tombstone communing with the dead like the devil's phantasm.

We look at Abigail and she has this dazed, faraway look in her huge Bambi eyes. I mean, we're used to her being a little distant maybe, but this is different. Who knows what mysteries of life and death this child has just witnessed beyond the veil. She may have been transported briefly into the afterlife. She may have been beamed up by aliens. She may be an alien exactly right now.

My dad looks at us and goes, "Do *not* tell your mother."

We're thinking, "Sure. Mom will totally not notice that her only daughter radiates light like the girl from *Poltergeist*. Our lips are sealed."

(For the record, my mom wants it stated that she did eventually figure out that Abigail walked by herself among various graves. Possibly due to the many church families who were gossiping about it that Sunday. She also wants it known that this incident is not to be confused with another time my sister was forgotten in a pumpkin patch on Halloween while dressed as Tinkerbell. Possibly because my family has issues.)

Me and Derek of course loved our little sister. And we showed our love by messing with her. I mean, honestly, I look back on those days and I think, "Where were Child Services? Shouldn't they have been protecting this girl?" Then I blame Derek for all of it.

We would get into these pillow fights, and me and Derek would just deck her. Like over and over and over. Right in the head. Part of it was that we were siblings, and that's what siblings do—they fight, they play rough, no matter what the age. It's how you bond. Part of it was that Abby actually wanted to be included in whatever we did. If me and Derek were in a pillow fight, she'd go, "Me too!" So we'd whack her in the head a whole bunch. I mean, she liked it. I think.

Did I mention this was all Derek's fault?

Christmas Day arrived, and I went to open my present from my sister. I mean, I didn't exactly have high hopes after the tie for my dad and the busted video game for my brother. But I tore open the paper, and there it was. A gift on a whole other level. My very own DVD of *Men in Black*.

First thing I thought was, "Huh. A movie about aliens. Maybe they *did* pick Abby up in that cemetery. It would explain so much."

Then I looked over at my sister, and she had tears in her eyes. I don't mean silent, dignified tears. I mean, straight-up little-girl crying. I had no idea what was going on. I had just opened this present! Which of course was wrapped in wrapping paper from Walmart! I didn't even have a chance to say thank you! What did I do wrong?

"I *know*!" she said through her sobs. "I *know* you said you hated it!"

Then it hit me—she'd overheard what I said to Derek the night before.

Man, I felt so awful. My heart just melted. The truth was I loved my little sister more than anything. I mean, maybe I hit her with a pillow a few times, but they were very, very soft pillows. And we left her behind once or twice, maybe three times, but we always got her back. *Eventually.*

I'd loved Abigail since the day she was born. When she was little, I'd rock her to sleep. When she got a little older, we'd sneak into the nearby golf course together and run around. We'd go sledding in the mud together in the winter. When I drove her around in my car with the tennis ball stick shift, we'd play CDs from her favorite Disney movies and just blast that stuff. *Little Mermaid* and *Lion King* and whatever, just screaming out the words at the top of our lungs, her as Ariel and Nala and me as Sebastian and Simba, which I know sounds kinda weird but I swear it's not. To this day, those are the only song lyrics I actually know.

I knelt down and gave my little sister a hug. I had to think fast. Which is generally something I'm not very good at.

"Abby," I said, "the only reason I said I hated it was because I was nervous no one would get it for me, so I was just pretending I didn't like it. But I love *Men in Black*!"

"Really?" she said, wiping the tears out of her eyes.

"Yeah, totally," I said. "Come on, let's me and you watch it right now."

So that's what we did. We sat down and we watched *Men in Black* on DVD right then and there. Honestly? It's a pretty good flick. I can't even tell you why I said I hated it so much when Derek asked me. I was just being a dumb teenager who thought I'd sound cool if I hated everything.

After that, I went all out for my sister. I was gonna prove my undying love for both her and cute CGI aliens no matter what. Me and Abby went to see every *Men in Black* sequel. We kept watching as Tommy Lee Jones got older and Will Smith got less cool in his Ray-Bans. We even rode the Men in Black ride at Universal together.

I figured I was doing it for Abigail. It made me happy knowing I was bringing my kid sister joy.

Then we watched the last movie. The one no one else watched. The one where they swapped everyone out for Tessa Thompson and Thor, for reasons I still don't understand. We laughed when we were supposed to laugh, we ate our Sour Patch Kids—well, *my* Sour Patch Kids, because I ate the whole box—and we had a good ol' time.

We left at the end, and Abigail goes, "Hey. You know I hate these movies, right?"

And I go, "Huh?"

"I hate these movies. Aliens? Pugs in sunglasses? It's just dumb. I only go because it makes you happy."

"But it only makes me happy because it makes you happy."

"Oh," she says. "Well, I guess we gotta keep going then."

"All right," I say. "I guess we do."

Yep. Totally should've left her in that cemetery.

THE BALLAD OF OLD BLUE

When I was sixteen I asked my parents if I could have a car.

My high school was a small blue-collar school called Donelson Christian Academy. My class had fifty students in it, and most of them had gone there their whole lives. I, on the other hand, had gone to public school until the ninth grade, when my dad got a job at Donelson as a teacher. Which got us a break on tuition, and also eventually led to me being cut from the basketball team by my own dad.

Don't worry, I've let it go. Even though I basically wrote a whole chapter about it later on.

So I was always kind of the new guy at school, at least compared to everyone else. Sure, I got to know people and make lots of friends, most of whom I still talk to to this day. But at first it was a little intimidating. Donelson was like most high schools. There were the kids who had the cool cars in the parking lot, and the kids who didn't. And I was like most teenagers. I wanted to be a kid with a cool car.

Specifically, I wanted a brand-new 1997 Chevy Camaro. One of the popular kids at school drove one, and I couldn't believe how awesome it was. It had the new body type, and it was long and sleek and shiny and black. This thing sparkled. I mean, I don't know how paint that's black can sparkle, but somehow this Camaro pulled it off.

Instead, my parents found me a 1985 Mazda 626 that someone parked on their front lawn with one of those "For Sale by Owner" signs for $1,500. It had sixty thousand miles on it. The crank-handle windows would get off their track, so you had to really jam them up there. And the stick shift was sticky to the touch, so I put a tennis ball over the knob to keep my hand not-gross. One time I was at a McDonald's drive-thru—I know, surprise—and the pretty girl at the window said she liked the tennis ball on the stick shift. I said thank you, but I'm pretty sure she just looked at the rest of that hunk of junk and thought, "This guy really needs a compliment. Just something to get him through the day." Also, my car was blue. Not a royal blue or even a powder blue, but the blue of old blue jeans that have been washed and stained and rewashed about a thousand times, until you can barely even tell they're still pants.

So basically, a Camaro.

I was a very good driver. My driver's ed had been taught by the high school football coach, Coach Wade, mostly I think because our school realized that being a football coach was not a full-time job. *Does the guy know how to drive? All right, try that. Better than teaching AP Physics.* He was firm but patient. This was helpful because the car we used didn't have a second safety brake for the instructor, because I am from the 1900s and we didn't like safety.

"Push the brake," he'd say. "Push the brake. PUSH THE BRAKE." Then we'd crash into a drainage ditch in someone's front yard—and then the kid pushed the brake.

My parents had to teach me to drive a stick shift, which is the closest I've ever come to being disowned. I remember practicing in our church parking lot. It was so jerky. I'd pop the clutch, the car would die, and my mom and dad would lose their minds. They'd go inside the church, say a prayer, come back out, and we'd do it over again. And over again. And over again. After all that, my parents earned a one-way ticket to

Heaven, but I still decided to take my driver's test using my aunt Judy's automatic. It took me three tries to pass the written portion, so I didn't want to take any chances with the driving part.

My last influence was Miss Woods, who worked at our school and drove me home sometimes. She was old and tiny, and she drove a Buick so big she could barely reach the pedals, so she drove with both feet— right on the gas, left on the brake. I saw this one day, and I thought, yeah, why wouldn't you do that? Give each foot a job, it seems so logical. To this day, I drive with both my feet. And surprisingly most people don't care for that.

But being a good driver wasn't enough for me. Okay, so maybe I didn't own anything as cool as a black Camaro, but I needed something— something—to make my car stand out. Something to make it special. Something to make it famous at my small Christian school in my small Tennessee town. So I decided to give it a name. I called it . . . Old Blue.

I mean, it was old and it was blue. So yeah. Seemed like the smart choice.

Of course, just giving my car a name wasn't enough.

Whatever I called it, it was still a clunky Mazda with a tennis ball for a stick shift. So I started a whole campaign. A charm offensive, if you will. So that people thought of my car not just as another car, but almost like a fun-loving character in the action of our teenage lives.

If me and my buddies were all gonna drive somewhere, and they were in their own superior automobiles, I'd shout, "All right, I'm bringing Old Blue!" or "Old Blue will be right on your tail!" And sure, maybe he was on their tail because something was presently wrong with his engine, and he maxed out at thirty-five miles per hour, but still—Old Blue was there.

I was never embarrassed of him, never ashamed. If anything, it was the opposite. I'd head to a party and make sure to park my car right at the front, right next to the cool-kid cars, the Mustangs and the Corvettes and even that shiny black Camaro. Old Blue wasn't afraid of any man, beast, or vehicle. He didn't yield for any oncoming traffic, even, at times, when he technically did not have the right of way.

And you know what? Over time, my campaign started to work. I kept parking Old Blue right at the front of every event we attended, and eventually he was not only accepted but welcomed. If some new guy was like, "Whose car is *that*?" everyone would give him a knowing look and be like, "That's Old Blue, dude. He's allowed here amongst all these other cars."

One day, me and Old Blue got into a fender bender with a very popular girl named Britney, when we accidentally rear-ended her brand-new Saturn. And this was back when Saturns were really Saturns. Nothing close to the Camaro, but still a very nice car. How exactly the crash happened with me using both feet remains a mystery. It's obviously such a foolproof method of driving. But it happened, and I must admit that even my confidence in the worthiness of my car was shaken in the face of this attractive cheerleader.

After the crash, we drove our cars back to her place so her dad could take a look. I was so nervous, just sick to my stomach. She lived in this nice neighborhood with all these big, new houses. Nothing like where I lived. I got out of my car and walked up to her front door, my knees shaking worse than Old Blue in fifth gear, and you know what? Her dad was absolutely fine about the whole thing. Totally nice, totally relaxed.

And yeah, it was probably because there was not a *scratch* on her Saturn. I mean, those black plastic bumpers, man—everything bounced right off.

But I like to think he took one look at my car, with its big fresh dent in its rusty metal bumper, and said to himself, "All good. It's Old Blue."

There's something about having a run-down clunker like that, especially when you're a kid. With a fancy new car, everything comes easy. You can take it for granted.

You can never take anything for granted with an old car. You appreciate it, you take pride in who and what you are. Every time you turn the key in the ignition and that thing starts, you say a little prayer of thanks. Every time you make it through the drive-thru without stalling, that chocolate shake tastes extra sweet.

I could take you to the exact spot where me and Old Blue hit a hundred thousand miles. I was less than a minute from my house, just me and my car, and I slowed down so I could savor every click of the odometer as it reached 1-0-0-0-0-0. It was a rite of passage. A huge deal. I mean, at that point, I never thought I would accomplish anything in my life. I wasn't on a path of big accomplishments. I never thought too much ahead at all. But you know what? Me and my car had done a hundred thousand miles together. That was quite the achievement.

Well, forty thousand, given that it already had sixty when I got it. But who's counting?

When I got older and computer passwords became a thing, what do you think was my go-to? That's right—it was that symbol of my youth, that foundation of my identity, that key to who I was. For every single account I owned, no matter what—email, bank card, AOL, Xbox, whatever—every password was OldBlue.

Actually, now that I think about it, I started with "oldblue," all lowercase. Then all of a sudden the computer people, whoever runs that stuff, were like, "Nope, you need better security, gotta add some capitals." So I was like, fine, OldBlue. Next thing I knew they wanted numbers. Well, Old Blue was a Mazda 626, so I went with OldBlue626. Then they're like, "Gotta get a special character!" So I'm like, "Golly, that's ridiculous!"

And every single one of my passwords, to this day, is OldBlue626#. And now, I will have to change them all. Bye-bye, foundation of my identity.

My daughter will be able to drive in a few years, and I'm sure she'll want something fancier than what I had. I mean, these days even if a kid is driving a Toyota Corolla it's always a 2025 model. When I grew up, if someone drove a Corolla you can bet your life it was no newer than

1989. But something's happened to all the old cars. It's like they're just *gone*. Like the auto industry got together and all said, "You know what? We're tired of today's youth having character and values. Get rid of all the old vehicles! Flood the market with shiny new Corollas! And get rid of stick shifts while you're at it. No more parents praying for their sanity in church parking lots. *Automatics for everyone!*"

But I don't care what my daughter says, she's getting an old car. I'm not saying it has to be blue. Let's not get crazy. You could come up with a decent name from yellow. Or, I guess, yeller. Also green. Or red. Probably not purple or mauve, which I actually do not know how to pronounce. But her car does have to be old. I will not bend on that.

Also it needs antilock brakes. Also airbags that cover literally every single inch of the interior and are ideally always inflated at all times, like bubble wrap. Also the most advanced, high-tech, state-of-the-art seatbelt system that science has ever created, preferably with futuristic safety things that are not even yet available to other people, but have been specially released only to my precious baby girl.

But still. Old. Very old. That is definitely the way to go.

My senior year of high school, I was voted homecoming king. Me, the former new kid. I still have no idea how this occurred. My best guess is that I was apparently not the only one in our education system who had trouble counting.

Or maybe I was a little like Old Blue. A little busted, a little creaky. I didn't do the things the popular kids did. I didn't drink. I didn't cuss. I got cut from the basketball team every year. I had never won a thing in my life. But maybe that wasn't so bad. I never got pigeonholed. No one defined me—I defined myself. So I got to be friends with everyone, no matter what sports they played, no matter how old they were, no matter what clique they were in.

The day before the homecoming game, there was a big pep rally. As part of the festivities, the school put on a spoof of *Love Connection*.

A little edgy for a Christian school, I know, but when it comes to celebrating football in the South all bets are pretty much off. One of the very first questions was who the female contestants would rather go out with—a guy who drove a black Camaro, or someone who drove Old Blue.

My brain nearly exploded.

They had just mentioned the Camaro I'd always dreamed of—so sleek, so shiny, so cool—in the exact same sentence as Old Blue. Even though its windows hardly rolled up. Even though the sticky stick shift was covered with a fuzzy green tennis ball. Even though there was now a big dent on the hood, which still seriously baffles me because driving with both feet really is very safe. They put Old Blue head-to-head against a brand-new black Camaro, and no one even thought twice. Old Blue officially had his rep. People knew who he was.

I mean, sure, the girls all picked the Camaro. Didn't even hesitate for half a second. Just blurted out, "*The Camaro! Not Old Blue!*" But still, they knew his name.

Me and my buddy Travis back in high school.
I can't believe the girl contestants passed on face-paint guy.

A few months later, I graduated. I swear I did, but please don't check those transcripts. It was finally time to part ways with Old Blue. Someone else was in need of his services, some friends of our family who lived down in Texas. We weren't rich people, far from it. But we gave it to our buddies for free. They were looking for a first car, just like I'd been, and we knew the special kind of impact Old Blue could have on a young life.

Plus, if I'm being honest, Old Blue was basically done by that point, all spewing fumes and making these weird grinding noises, and no one would've actually paid us for it, so it was like—hey, be our guest. I do believe I recall hearing somewhere that Old Blue cracked two hundred thousand miles, though that may have just been a dream.

For my next car, I got a hand-me-down from my mom. Her 1989 Honda Civic. It still had the jerky crank-handle windows, and the tint on the back window was all bubbly because we got it done cheap. But it was four years younger than Old Blue, so that was something. It was also blue. So I called it New Blue.

Somehow, it never had the same ring.

THE PERFECT SOCK

It is very complex to simplify your life.

To me, the dumb little decisions are always the hardest ones. I have no problem with the big decisions. Do we need a second mortgage on our house? Easy. Whatever my wife says a second mortgage is, that is the answer. Should our child go to school? Probably. But the little things? I need those to be solved before I can move on, and if they aren't solved I will totally not move on.

Like socks. Who are these animals out there, just waking up in the morning and throwing on socks with no planning whatsoever? It makes no sense! They're just reaching into their sock drawers all willy-nilly, they're grabbing whatever they can find, they're mixing colors and textures and fabrics. They're wearing polyester on one foot and cotton on the other. They're blending Nike and Reebok, when everyone knows that those two brands do not get along. A Nike sock and a Reebok sock are like *Romeo and Janet*. I know it's Juliet, but I just wanted to show the insanity of Nike + Reebok to me. It is chaos.

But I don't just need my socks to match. I need my socks to be the right socks, or I will think about nothing else for the rest of the day.

Will my socks stay firmly pulled up around my calves, or will they start to slip down in the middle of an important conversation? Because that would be very distracting if I ever had an important conversation. What about cushioning? Will my socks provide enough cushioning for the soles of my feet? Because my feet play a pretty big part in my day-to-day. How about sweat wicking? Will my socks wick my sweat in an effective fashion, or will they not be as wickery as I want them to be? Could they be too wickery? These are important matters I need answers to.

Someone please make me the world's first perfect sock, and I guarantee you that will be the only sock I buy for the rest of my life. How many socks does a successful sock company need to sell in a year? Maybe twenty? That will be me. I will be your biggest customer, and I will spread the word about the greatness of your perfect sock far and wide, and you will sell at least ten more socks. I may even buy your company and become a sock CEO. This comedy thing is a fine job, but it does not provide simplicity for my feet.

Socks, of course, are not the only complex decision I face each day. I wore the same brown belt for twenty years. It fit. It worked. It did not rub my stomach weird or get caught between the folds in my skin. Recently, I started mixing two belts, which I feel is a real sign of progress on my part. Though it does take me at least ten minutes to decide between the two, and I usually ask my wife for help. One is brown, and one is even more brown, so you see the dilemma.

The thing is, I do like change. It just has to be a really specific kind of change. For a while all I wore was Nike. Nike hats, Nike shirts, Nike pants, Nike shoes. Nike was my thing. Then I decided I needed a change. So I made all my clothes Puma instead. Puma hats, Puma shirts, Puma pants, Puma shoes. That's my kind of change—change with a whole bunch of same.

To be clear, I do believe some brands can be worn together. But they cannot be competing brands. When I'm golfing I sometimes wear all

TravisMathew with Nike shoes. TravisMathew is a golf-wear brand, and Mr. Mathew is not offended by Nikes. But I wouldn't wear all Adidas clothes with Reebok shoes, for example. You could maybe talk me into New Balance shoes and Nike gear up top.

You know what? You can't. That's ridiculous. Too much stuff that starts with "n." Me, Nike, New Balance. Just can't do it.

The most simplicity would be to wear the same outfit every single day, all day long, from the moment I wake up until the moment I go to bed, and for no one to think that is strange. That is my dream. Like a not-smart Steve Jobs.

Sometimes I think I could wear a suit all day, every day. Some guys look really sharp in suits. Am I one of those guys? I don't know, because I've never worn one, but I guess we would find out. Then I start thinking about everything it would take to keep that up. To wear a suit when I'm golfing, while I'm watching TV, when I go to McDonald's. Does Nike even make suits? I don't know if suits even *have* brands.

Then I get overwhelmed. I then want to throw all my clothes away and start all over again from scratch. But I bet I would just end up buying the same stuff I already own.

THE TIME I MADE THE NBA

My senior year of high school it was my dream to play in the NBA. I even wrote it in my yearbook: *Where are you going to be in ten years? I, Nate Bargatze, will be playing in the NBA.*

'Course, everyone thought I was joking because I got cut every year from my high school team. My freshman year my dad was actually an assistant coach, and I still got cut. Which isn't easy on your pride, when it's your own father telling you you're not good enough to play basketball for a school called Donelson Christian Academy that only has two hundred students, and also your dad happens to be a magician and part-time clown named Yo-Yo.

So instead of my high school, I had to play for my church. Because I figured the church could not cut you. They have to let you play, right? Or I guess they could cut you, but you'd have to be pretty bad. Like, "Look, *we* think you're pretty good, but . . . Jesus does not think you're good. And Jesus is our captain."

Now, I wasn't actually a horrible player. I was definitely one of the best kids who couldn't make the real basketball team. I was quick, I could shoot threes. And I was money from the elbow. Like, you do not want me shooting from the elbow, because my shot is automatic from that one very small spot on the entire court.

Living the dream.

So Jesus was okay with my skills. I made the team. And turns out I did actually play for the NBA. The Nashville Baptist Association. So to all the haters out there who thought I couldn't do it—hey, joke's on you.

Church ball was a lot different.

We'd travel each week to play against other churches all over, not only Tennessee but Kentucky too. If there were semi-talented Christians somewhere in the South who wanted to participate in a game of competitive basketball, we were there. The courts we played on were very much up to NBA standards. The Baptist one, not the other one. Sometimes the gyms were so small, we only played half-court. Generally they did have at least one basket, so that was a plus. But there might not be a three-point line. Out of bounds would be running into the wall. And occasionally we also played on carpet.

Seriously. Like an actual, very big, gym-sized rug that would have free-throw lines and boundaries and everything painted right on. You can go online, right now, on your very own computer, and find these basketball-court carpets for sale, and you can buy one yourself. Even though they are carpet, they are "hard carpet," which I believe is a technical carpet term, so you really can bounce a ball on them. I'm not sure if they'll deliver them to nonbelievers above the Mason-Dixon Line, there may be some sort of geographical and cultural restrictions, but if you can get your hands on one they're easy to maintain. Just run a vacuum after every basket, maybe bring a lint roller, and you're good.

You might think that church games would be, like, holy. These mellow, turn-the-other-cheek contests where people just exchanged baskets and always agreed to end in a tie. Like, "Hey, we're all Christians here. Ain't we all winners at Judgment Day?"

Heck no. These church games were absolutely vicious. I mean *cutthroat* competitive. I honestly have no idea why. Maybe it was because everyone knew each other, so it made winning or losing feel personal. "Look at Dave dribbling that ball over there. That potato salad he brought to the potluck was so dry and flavorless. And that dude had the nerve to pass it off as homemade. Well, Dave, say hello to my elbow."

Maybe everyone just got sick and tired of being goody-goody during regular life, always having to be nice and polite no matter what, so they all decided to let loose and get crazy on the court. No holds barred, all the rules out the window. Like something out of *Hoosiers* meets *The Purge*. At best they'd follow maybe two or three of the Commandments if everyone was lucky.

The first time I saw a church-league game, I was appalled. Shellshocked. I was expecting a normal, spirited game of carpeted basketball, and instead I ended up hacking my way through the jungles of Vietnam.

The adult leagues were actually the worst. I saw grown men, pillars of their community, cheating, shouting at the refs, getting into fistfights, and using language that stunned my young ears.

Was Pastor Mike speaking in tongues? The worst thing I'd ever heard him say before was "That's a stinker." But this didn't even sound like English. Maybe it was some ancient language from a lost book of the Bible. Either way, he should probably keep that out of his Sunday sermon.

They'd do whatever it took to win. They'd stack these church teams with ringers, just load them up with talent. You'd have a bunch of guys who were normal members of the congregation, regular shmoes like everyone else. Then you'd see this absolute giant of a man, maybe six-foot-eight, and you'd find out he used to be a D-III college player or maybe he had a cup of coffee once with the Bucks, and they shipped him in from Milwaukee just for this game. Like, was this dude even Christian?

And the coach would say, "Whatever, have you seen his spin move? That's plenty of religion for me. Now get out there and take no prisoners."

Then at the end of every game, after the ambulance had left and they wet vac-ed all the blood off the court, everyone would meet up in the center and pray. "Dear Heavenly Father, please forgive us for everything that just happened here in this place. It was an abomination, and we didn't mean any of it. Although, Pastor Mike, there's no way that last shot was a three. We all saw your foot on the line. All of us, including God. Amen."

Not just basketball, by the way. Pretty much any church sports league was like *Mad Max Beyond Thunderdome*. If you couldn't get out your frustrations on the hardwood, there were plenty of opportunities for bloodthirsty fellowship. Softball, you'd see those dugouts clear a couple times a week. Whole squads just brawling. Co-ed teams too. Men, women, husbands, wives, all turning the pitcher's mound into a mosh pit. Bowling, you watch out for those ugly shoes. You can fit a switch-blade on the toes of those things. And football? Honestly, I think they pretty much avoided tackle football. People knew that actual, physical deaths—straight-up homicide—would result.

Some things you just can't take back.

And at first I didn't get it. Why was everyone getting so crazy about these games? I mean, the stakes were literally zero. You won nothing. Sometimes it was actually worse than nothing. You'd look at the tiny plastic trophy covered in fake gold paint that someone picked up for $4.99 at Walmart, and it would be like, "No seriously—you keep that. You go right ahead and take that golden metallic Smurf on a plywood base home with you."

But then I started playing church basketball myself. And before I knew it, I was sucked in. Don't get me wrong—I was still having fun. I wasn't one of those guys who took it so seriously that I made myself miserable. But my whole life up to then had been nothing but pickup games with buddies, just grabbing a court at a park and having fun. Now I was playing in a real official game, on a real, organized team, with actual timed games on hardwood or on carpet—and, dude, I was *in it*. Tripping, throwing body blocks, talking trash. "Don't let me get to that elbow! You know what'll happen! That elbow is *mine*, game over!

" . . . Okay, fine, yes, I realize that all you have to do is basically stand at the elbow, stationary, to prevent me from getting to the one spot that I can hit a basket from, but still. Don't you let me get to that elbow!"

Were there real stakes? Who cared?

One of our biggest games of all time took place at this church in Kentucky. We showed up to play and it just so happened to be *the* home church of one of the stars of MTV's *Real World*. And I'm not talking about season 53, when no one really cares and everyone's too busy watching *Floor Is Lava* on Netflix. No, this was *Real World: Los Angeles*, the second season, when reality TV was still new and people actually thought MTV had come up with some amazing social experiment that could totally change the world, which also came on right after its spring break special with all the girls in bathing suits. I watched it, you watched it, we all watched it, and we didn't even have to pretend we didn't watch it, that's how exciting it was.

Real World was a big deal, and in the bleachers that day was one of its biggest stars, Jon Brennan. You know the one I'm talking about—the country music singer they threw into the mix, with his twang and his cowboy hat and his glorious golden mullet. This guy was one of us. Just another Jesus-loving Southern boy spending the day at a Baptist gym. Except for one massive difference. He was famous. And that was cool.

Let me tell you, I went crazy that game. Man, I balled out. I warned them too. I told those kids from Kentucky not to let me get to that elbow. *I told them!* Did they listen? Nope.

I was scoring from the left elbow. I was scoring from the right elbow. I even hit a couple shots from other non-elbow areas of the basketball court. I finished that game with a career-high nineteen points, six assists, and three rebounds. We mopped the floor with those Christians from Kentucky. Beat 'em by twelve points. Showed no mercy. Wasn't even close.

Did it matter? Not in the slightest.

Here's how little it mattered. I actually have no idea how many points I scored that game. No one kept stats. They barely kept score. Nineteen? I made it up. Sounded good at the time. By which I mean literally at the very moment I typed out "nineteen" just a few seconds ago. It sounds more impressive than twelve, but not as unbelievable as twenty-six. I mean, that would've just been arrogant.

Six assists and three rebounds? Could've been. Feels about right.

Even the Jon Brennan part is a little hazy, to be fair. I mean, someone from the *Real World* was definitely at that game. Definitely. I think. Could've been Puck. Maybe Kevin. Wait, he was *New York*, wasn't he.

Honestly, that'd be kind of crazy—Puck or Kevin at a Baptist church basketball game in Kentucky. So it was probably Jon.

But I'm 99 percent sure we won that game. Well, 98. Give or take. And I absolutely played one of my best games there. I guarantee you I impressed . . . whoever from the *Real World* was watching.

So, yeah. Totally meaningless. I mean, it was *church basketball*. No matter how hard we played, no matter how serious we took it at the time, of course it was meaningless. The trophy cost less than gas money to the games. But that's kind of the point. That's what I realized. The biggest games, the most fun I ever had playing basketball—or any sport really—were always the most meaningless. Always.

Some of the toughest, hardest-fought games I played were against myself in my backyard in Old Hickory, Tennessee. I'd be back there for eight hours at a time, going one-on-one against my imagination. In my mind, I was always down one, and the clock was always counting down to the very last seconds of the game. The crowd was chanting my name, I had enough time to get off one last shot, and probably I was overcoming an injury. Nothing too major, just a missing foot or two, but something super heroic so everyone would shake their heads and say, "Wow, we wish we could be that brave." I'd get the ball, I'd hobble down the court, I'd shoot—and somehow, some way, I always won.

Okay, every now and then I did lose. I did. But for some reason it never hurt quite as bad when my opponent was me. That guy had a heck of a crossover.

Then there was gym class. You couldn't get any more pointless than that.

By the time I got to my senior year, it felt like everyone I knew was taking AP courses. AP Calculus, AP Chemistry, AP Physics—everything AP, everyone getting ready for their big, advanced dreams out in the big, advanced post–high school world. Except for me. After four years, I was still taking all the most basic classes. And that included gym, a course almost everybody else finished off when they were fourteen.

But that was fine. Me and my senior buddies in gym just decided to call it AP Wellness. Maybe we weren't earning any college credit, but we did PE at a very advanced level. Freshmen and other younger students in the class were allowed to take part in our activities, but only in supporting roles, like handing us the occasional towel to wipe off our older, dumber foreheads. The basketball games we played, all between the lowest achievers in our school, were some of the most epic battles you've ever seen.

One game got so crazy, we even called time-out. Now, you might be asking, how do you call time-out at the end of a game where the only clock is just an *actual* clock? Like, when class is over, the game is over, right? That's it. It's done. You can't stop time.

But we did. Yes, we did.

We had about a minute to go before the end of class, we were down one point, the action was intense, and we looked at our PE teacher and shouted, "TIME-OUT!"

Our teacher thought about it. I can't tell you what exactly went through his brain. Possibly it was, "What's the worst that can happen? They're late for Basic Reading? These boys oughta live for the now."

Either way, he gave us that time-out. And time did stop. Or maybe it kept going, but we just ended up being late for Basic Reading. I honestly can't remember. But what I can remember is that after that time-out, we needed a hero. Someone to get us the W. Someone who had practiced countless last-second shots in his own backyard. Someone who had won all of those games against himself. Or at least a lot of them.

And that hero was not me.

It was one of my friends, a kid named Jeremy who everyone called P-P because once when he was playing football, someone threw the ball and hit him in the . . . well, you know the story.

But a few extra details won't hurt. When it happened, he was a very small freshman doing drills on the freshman team, and one of the coaches shouted, "Turn!" So P turned, and they threw the ball at that section.* It was the mid-nineties. Different time for coaches back then.

P, as you might guess, was not exactly gifted in basketball. His one job on our gym team was to pass the ball immediately to anybody else, possibly myself, because I was, after all, one of the best kids who couldn't make the real basketball team.

But when it's time for our team to pass the ball inbounds, everyone else is covered. I'm double-teamed, because, you know, they aren't going to let me get to that elbow. The last few seconds of the only overtime game in the history of AP Wellness are ticking down. Ticking. Ticking. Ticking. And the ball's gotta go somewhere.

So it goes to P. And what does he do? He just chucks it. Just flings the ball with all of his might, with this awful form, over his shoulder. I don't even know if P had his eyes open for this last-second shot, at best he was squinting with one eye, that's how crazy it is. And it goes in. Right when the school's second bell rings, telling us we should already be in the next class reading at a very low level, that basketball goes through the hoop. And we win.

We all go nuts. Screaming, jumping up and down, tackling P in the middle of the court, like this is the greatest thing that's ever happened in the history of the world. No one else is even watching, no one else is even there. It's only us and the PE teacher, who's probably thinking, "Maybe gym is too intellectually challenging for these guys."

Now, I'm still friends with P to this day. In fact, I still call him P. Though to be clear, "P" is reserved for close friends, while the more formal "P-P" is used by people who don't know him as well, like my mom and dad. Me and P both have families now. This dude has children of his own. He's a grown man. And he's still living down a nickname he got in high school when he was hit by a football in the you-know-what.

---

* That's what happens when you don't curse. You say stuff kinda weird.

But whenever I call him P—and I do, in front of his kids, and they love it—whenever we're laughing or poking fun at each other, he can still turn to me, look me dead in the eye, and say, "Yeah, but I won us that game in gym class that day on a last-second three."

And I say, "Yeah, P. Yeah, you did."

All right, so maybe I never did make it into the *big* NBA. The one that's about Basketball and not just Baptists. But so what? Me and my buddies didn't have to be pros to love to play. When we played those silly games, we got a chance to be bigger than ourselves. For one shining moment, we got a chance to be great. That's all that really mattered.

And if you didn't get that "one shining moment" reference, there is a very good chance you have not understood a word of this entire chapter.

A couple years ago, I was able to give some money to my old high school. I still love the place, and it's not like any college can or would want to call me an alumni. But Donelson Christian Academy is proud to have me, and as thanks they were even nice enough to put my name on the court. No joke, painted right there on the floor, which thankfully is not carpeted, it now says "The Nate Bargatze Basketball Court." The very court I was cut from all four years.

Now every time someone attends a game, they can look at my name and ask, "Wow, how great a player was Nate back when he went here?"

And the school will then say, "Not very good. But don't you let him get to the elbow. He is automatic from that one spot."

I told them to say that last part.

I'M IN YOUR HEAD

My brother Derek is not better than me at anything. But he pretends he's better than me at everything, which is what makes him one of the most annoying people in the world.

A few years ago, back when I was twenty and he was seventeen—so technically adults—our family went down to Louisville for a big Thanksgiving with my mom's extended family. We hadn't seen them for a million years, and it was kind of like a reunion. So the stakes were high, right? You want to make a good impression so by the time you leave, they're like, "Wow, even *we're* embarrassed we live in Kentucky."

Plus, we were born-again Christians, but because my mom's relatives didn't go to church five times a week like us, we all thought they'd lost their way. Obviously it was up to us to set a good example and get them back on the straight and narrow. So naturally the first thing me and my brother said to our cousins is, "Wanna play Spades?"

Sure, this was one step away from high-stakes gambling and a life of crime, but we were riding with God, so it was cool. The opening bet was five bucks and the keys to your soul.

Our cousins agreed to our sinful little game, but it was about to get worse than they could possibly imagine. Because what they didn't know was that me and my brother are basically crazy. Specifically, we're crazy when it comes to competing with each other.

I'm three years older than Derek, so he was literally born in second place. I love the guy, but that's just a fact. I've heard that second children are usually the wild ones, and first children are responsible, but in our case the roles were very switched. He was so goody-goody that in high school he was actually, no joke, voted "Most Christ-like." *Twice*. What does that even *mean*? I graduated before he started, so I wasn't around to, like, bear witness. Was he just kissing up to all the teachers, or was my brother actually walking down the halls curing leprosy and performing miracles on pop quizzes? Did he try out for the football team in a robe and sandals? Because that's actually kind of impressive.

I, on the other hand, was voted Homecoming King, because I was fun and people liked me. Kind of its own miracle, I guess, but it seemed to work out okay.

If for some reason you've been paying attention, you'll remember that we did have a younger sister, Abigail, but my parents had her seven years after Derek, so me and my brother were really raised as a twofer. And as far as our dad was concerned, he was raising his two boys to be warriors. But not even cool warriors. I mean warriors in the dumbest way possible. Which makes sense when you remember he was a professional clown and magician.

Everything was a competition. Everything was a lesson about how tough life was. Even if we were lucky enough to do something fun—nothing fancy, just going to a swimming pool for the day, something normal people who do normal fun things take for granted—we could never actually enjoy it. There was no hanging out and being lazy floating on a raft. Nope, as soon as we dipped one toe into that water, my dad would shout out, "All right! I'm gonna throw this giant rock into the deep end! Let's see who can bring it back first!"

And I'd be like, "But, Dad, I can barely swim! Derek is still wearing floaties on his arms! How are we supposed to get some huge rock out of the deep end?"

My dad would go, "Let me tell y'all something—*life* is the deep end. You think life cares if you can swim? There are no floaties in *life*! Now go on and get that rock!"

Then he would squeeze his bright red clown nose and do a card trick. And I would beat my brother in his floaties, because I am older and also naturally better.

When I was ten and Derek was seven, my dad actually bought us three boxing gloves—three—so that one of us would get the unfair advantage of fighting with only one hand. There is also a chance that we just lost one of the gloves, but it's more fun to blame my dad. At the time, I was bigger and stronger than my little brother, so I let Derek have the two gloves, while I fought with one hand. He then got me with a right hook that was so hard it knocked out a silver filling from my tooth, because I was born in the 1900s and wooden teeth had just been banned. For the record, though, I still won the fight, because I was born first, and that's just how it goes.

As we grew up, though, something strange happened. I stayed older, but my little brother started to get taller than me. He eventually grew taller than me by two inches. Or as I like to call it, "the same height." This was a jarring experience, because it was so against the natural order of things. And because it meant I had to stand on my tiptoes whenever we hung out, just to keep him in check. It also became apparent that he was actually pretty good at sports. Basketball. Baseball. Golf. Was he better than me? Absolutely not. But coincidentally it was right around this time that I started to focus more on board games.

Again, my dad had done a great job showing us the worst way to compete. When we were little, he taught both me and Derek how to play checkers and chess, or as I call it, "educated checkers." And our dad would only play us straight-up. He absolutely refused to let his

My dad had giant bunnies training us in hand-to-hand combat.

children win. So you'd have this grown man sitting there, staring at the board with his forehead all wrinkled, thinking for ten minutes before he made each move, and then he'd finally go, "Checkmate." And I'd say, "Okay, Dad. You beat me, I guess." I hadn't even mastered Go Fish. But congrats, dude.

My mom would watch this and she'd be horrified. Like, "Steve, you're being mean! It's *mean* to beat your kids like this!"

He'd go, "*Life* is mean! They need to learn that now before it's too late!"

"They're three and six," she'd say. "I think they've got time."

She could've added, "And you're a professional clown," but she preferred to pull her punches.

Eventually, after years and years, my brother and I each finally managed to beat my dad. And then he never played us again. He was like, "I've taught you well, my sons. Now it's finally time for you to go forth and face each other in this game called life." I mean, that's what he said. Mostly I think it just wasn't fun for him to lose to little kids.

So by the time me and Derek got to this family reunion in Louisville, cards weren't just cards. Spades weren't just Spades. It was a battle for honor. A battle for respect. A battle for dignity. And in the Bargatze household there was almost none of that to go around. So pretty much a battle to the death.

Almost everyone was down in the basement in the family room. The TV was on with a football game or something. My grandpa, who was deaf and barely remembered our names, was smoking a cigar. My mom was trying to get him to hear her. My dad was actually upstairs because he'd just had the first of many hernia surgeries and couldn't do steps. And me and my cousin were going up against Derek and another cousin.

Now, if you don't know the rules to Spades, I am here to tell you that that doesn't matter. All you need to know is that I am the king of Spades, and that my team was absolutely destroying my brother's team in a way that was very satisfying. Hand after hand. Game after game. I was winning. Because that is nature and it is right.

Then my brother did something. He did something only he knows how to do. He got under my skin.

It sincerely hurts me to admit that he can do this. As I am writing these words, I am experiencing actual physical pain somewhere below my neck and above my stomach, right behind my back. In fact, I would probably call the doctor except that I have experienced this pain before and it is my brother.

Other people can get under my skin, of course, but my brother is uniquely good at it. He has developed this tactic over a lifetime of constantly losing to me at everything. It's kind of a coping mechanism. Sure, he's coming in second, but at least he can drive me completely bonkers in the process. It is the one and only way I will actually admit he has me beat, though now that I think about it I can't let him know that, so I will probably remove this entire chapter from the copy of this book I make him buy.

Most annoying of all, he doesn't get under my skin by being angry or yelling or getting excited like a normal competitive person. He does it by tapping into the same second-child smarts and responsibility that have always made him so irritating. He does it by being calm. Calm and cool in the most irritating way you can imagine. With this cool, calm, satisfied little smile that is basically the worst thing in the universe.

Me and my cousin had just beat Derek and our other cousin—again— when out of nowhere my little brother reached his hand into the pile of discarded cards, got that little smile on his face, picked up a card, and very calmly, very coolly, said, "Oh. We discarded this on accident, but this is the card we meant to play. So actually we won this game."

Now, let's just stop and think about this for a second, all right? What my brother said blatantly made no sense. *No. Sense.* I mean, they had *discarded* the card! It wasn't even in play! It was literally out of the game! Arguing over whether or not it counted was like arguing over whether or not a car was red or green. You can't even argue over it—it just is!

But he gets that stupid little smile, he gets that calm little stupid voice, and I just have to say it. I have to. I have no choice. "You did not win this game, okay?"

"Yes, we won the game." *He said it so dang calm!*

"No. You. Didn't."

"Yes, we did." *He was so dang cool!*

"You can't do that! YOU CAN'T DO THAT!"

"It's okay, we can do that." *He had that stupid little smile!*

And because this is all happening in front of our long-lost family members who we are desperately trying to impress with our holiness, I decide it is necessary to escalate matters.

"OUTSIDE!" I shout. "We are taking this outside, right now!"

"Okay," goes my smiling little brother. "We can take this outside."

I jump out of my seat. My brother calmly rises from his. Our cousins' jaws drop.

"WHAT?" yells my deaf grandfather with the cigar. "DID SOMEONE SAY SOMETHING?"

"Stop it, boys!" my mom pleads. "We're the Christians! We're supposed to be the good ones!"

"This is life!" my dad calls down from upstairs. "THIS IS LIFE!"

Then I say it. The best, most perfect thing to say ever. The thing that is best and most perfect because it is so totally, so obviously true to everyone in the whole world.

"Dude," I say, "you will never beat me, because I am your older brother, and I am in your head. Every single day, no matter what, when you wake up, when you go to sleep, when you do anything, I am there, and I am in your head. I already won, because *I. Am. In. Your. Head.*"

And I see that cool little smile of his flicker. Just for a second. Because I'm his older brother and I will always be his older brother and he knows I'm right. I'm so right that we never even go outside to settle things man-to-man. What's the point? I'm already living in the guy's head.

Also, Derek really does have a mean right hook.

My little brother was never satisfied. It wasn't enough for him to drive me nuts. He had to get other people to join him. He even managed to turn my future wife against me.

I know what you're thinking. "Nate, how could your own flesh and blood do something so underhanded?" Well, I guess that just comes with the territory when you're voted "Most Christ-like" at our old high school. Though I do believe my alma mater should think of taking back at least *one* of his two titles.

This happened back when Laura was only my girlfriend. It was Christmas, and I brought her to my parents' house to meet my mom and dad and the whole family for the very first time, including Derek's wife and daughter, because he and I were supposedly adults at this point. And for some reason, someone made the brilliant decision for us to all play the board game Risk.

Once again, let's stop and think. Me and my brother almost came to blows over a simple game of cards. *Cards.* Risk, on the other hand, is a game that is literally about going to war. There's no mystery, there's no secret. There's no messing around with chutes or ladders or little squares with fake street names. Risk is world domination. Plain and simple. You roll some dice, you move around your troops, you take over Russia. It's pure, no-holds-barred aggression. But someone said, "Hey, let's do this! What better way to welcome Nate's new girlfriend to our absolutely insane family!"

So we all started playing, and as soon as we did I could tell something was up with Derek. Because I know Risk strategy, okay? Risk strategy is you want to take over the world. It's a very complex strategy, and it is perfect for my brain.

But instead of trying to take over the world like he should, my brother started coming after me. And only me. I had one infantry controlling this tiny little country of Siam, this territory no one even knows how to pronounce, and Derek went *out of his way* to attack me there. This dude was practically airlifting in troops from the Congo just to take out the little fruit stand I called a military base.

That would be bad enough, right? We all know that my brother can get under my skin. But then he tried to get Laura to gang up on me. He didn't nag her, never raised his voice—he just used that same calm, cool tone and that same annoying smile.

"Hey Laura, you're right by Iceland. Doesn't look like Nate's protecting it all that well. I bet you could conquer that one *real* easy."

What does Laura do? She goes along with it! Like, "Oh! I didn't even notice how vulnerable Nate's position is in Iceland. Thanks for pointing that out, Derek."

I mean, just a few minutes ago, these two hadn't even met, and now they're working together to undermine my whole geopolitical position. So I go, "You two can't gang up on me! There's no teams in Risk! *That's not allowed!*"

And Laura says, "That's not a rule! I can do what I want!"

So of course I say, "But it makes no sense! Clearly the most logical move is for you to attack Derek in the Congo! You're just doing what he wants!"

Then Derek, smiling his little smile, is like, "Nate, I really think our guest can make up her own mind. She seems quite intelligent."

And Laura says, "Nate, you're just mad because I'm beating you so bad."

But I'm not mad! I'm not mad at all! So I say, "I'm not mad! I'm not mad at all! But *you're* being an—"

Okay. Before I go any farther with this story, I want to talk a little bit about the meaning of the word "idiot" in my family. You might be thinking something like, "That's interesting, Nate. In your family does the word 'idiot' not mean a very stupid person?" But it does. It does.

However—and this is a very important "however"—when we call someone an idiot in my family, it is meant to be endearing. We are saying, "You are very stupid, but in a very adorable way." And you know what? That should count for something. That should count for a lot.

The roots of "idiot" as a term of endearment go way back in our family. I'm pretty well-known for being a "clean" comic, and no one in my family swears, at least the non-tatted ones. But when my dad grew up back in Kentucky, he and his family were a regular bunch of cussers. My mom also grew up in Kentucky, and she and her family were even bigger cussers. Does this say something about the state of Kentucky? I will allow you to draw your own conclusions. Also, yes, it does.

But when my dad eventually became born-again Christian and turned his life around, he gave up all the cussing—with two exceptions. The first is "dadgummit." No one really knows what it means or if it even qualifies as a swear word, but it's a lot of fun to say so my dad says it no less than ten times a day. It's kind of become an all-purpose word, like the word "Smurf" in the old *Smurfs* cartoon. You remember how they'd say, "We're about to Smurf over to the Smurf for a Smurfin' Smurf"? Well, that's what my father does with "dadgummit." It can be a noun or a verb or a, uh . . . other word-thingy too.

Number two is "idiot," which my dad and his brother called each other from back when they were little kids, so I guess it just managed to stick around. To him, it sounded a lot nicer than "stupid," which he called "the s-word."

A short while after my dad started dating my mom, he called her an idiot—no one can even remember why, that's how much he tosses it around—and she didn't even blink. Just called him an idiot right back. And that's how they knew it was true love. They have already informed us kids that on their tombstone they want it to say, "Here lies a couple idiots." Though to be fair to my mom, she was the bigger cusser back then, because, as she likes to put it, "I grew up Catholic." We still tell the story of when Mom was trying to assemble a cabinet, and she also said something much stronger than "dadgummit." Our jaws just dropped. "What is *happening* to our family? We are losing our mother to the devil."

That kind of leniency was never given to us kids. One afternoon, my brother rushed home to report to my mother that I had used "the f-word." Even my mom, with her sailor's mouth, was appalled. She then found out that Derek meant "fart." She laughed and was about to let me off, but then she decided she wasn't a fan of that f-word either. No reason why. She just wasn't. So we'd be sitting in the living room watching TV and we'd have to go, "Did someone just f-word in here?" We were always too scared to answer, and we didn't even understand why. Though I do understand why now, because as I have gotten older I don't care for that word either. I honestly don't even like talking about body stuff.

But "idiot"? That was just fine. We were baptized into its graces at a very young age. My dad told me and Derek to rake the leaves once. So we went outside to rake them—by just kind of spreading them to different parts of the yard, instead of putting them into one giant pile. My dad walks out, stares at us, and says, loud enough for us to hear, "Look at those idiots." Honestly, I don't even know who he was talking to. Who was he telling to look? Us? Our neighbors? God? Who? Anyway, me and Derek cried a little bit, but then we were like, "Well, he obviously means that to be endearing." And we never tried to rake the leaves again.

So now you understand exactly what I was trying to communicate to my someday-wife Laura when we were playing Risk that day. Unfortunately, though, she did not take it in the traditional Bargatze way.

Her face turns red, she jumps up from the chair, and she yells, "You will NEVER call me THAT WORD ever again!"

Derek, because he is super annoying, says, "You can't talk to her like that!"

My mom goes, "Laura, in our family, it's a term of endearment!"

I'm shouting, "I meant it endearing! I MEANT IT ENDEARING!"

Laura runs into the bathroom and slams the door behind her. My dad is so shocked he doesn't even say anything about life.

My mom sighs. "Well, you gotta marry her now."

That ended up being me and Laura's very first fight. I am very happy to say it was not our last one. I went after her, explained the history of profanity and the word "idiot" in our family, apologized over and over for what I said, and blamed Derek for everything. Looking back, it was the perfect way to welcome her to the Bargatzes.

I never called Laura "idiot" ever again, and my parents officially banned me and my brother from ever playing Risk. So of course me and Derek never competed over anything from then on.

That last thing I said? That was totally a lie.

As me and Derek got older, we stayed just as competitive as ever. We even tried to pass on our love of irrational conflict to our kids one Christmas a few years back.

Granted, his daughter Mayah was only ten and my girl Harper was nine, and yes, we could've just focused on Santa and presents. But you have probably noticed by now that for the Bargatzes, holidays are a time for hugs and also, maybe, knife fights. As my dad, the clown-magician of hard knocks, would put it, that's life in our family. Not at all controversial.

What *was* controversial that Christmas was that someone forgot to buy grape jelly for our big brunch at my parents' house. I mean, seriously, how were we supposed to have Christmas without grape jelly? The two essential staples at the Bargatze household are ketchup and grape jelly. I grew up with literal vats of the stuff in our fridge. I put it on everything. Now, I know some families are strawberry jelly people, and that's fine, I guess, but grape is the Bargatze jelly of choice. And we do jelly, not jam. Because we don't think we're better than anybody.

Well, that morning, someway, somehow, there was plenty of ketchup in the house but not a *speck* of grape jelly. The Bargatze men have a thing when it comes to condiments, and that was fine for my dad and brother, because they are both Ketchup Men. But I am a Grape Jelly Man, and ketchup might go fine on eggs, but it does *not* go on biscuits. I am a man of tradition. I am a man of taste. I am a man who does not like dry, crumbly biscuits on Christmas morning. So how in the heck was I supposed to have my Christmas biscuits without grape jelly? How??

To try to distract us (me) from this controversy, we naturally decided that the whole family should play some dice while my mom was cooking.

One more time, let's stop and think. Playing Spades almost sparked a fist fight. Risk almost broke up my marriage before it even got started. Whose brilliant idea was it to roll dice? Possibly mine, come to think of it, but I blame the lack of grape jelly.

The game was Grego,* where the way we play it, the first one who reaches a hundred points wins, but you drop down to zero if you hit snake eyes. Eventually, all of us got knocked out except for Mayah and Harper. And honestly, even at that point, even when it was my daughter and Derek's daughter going head-to-head, it was still just a nice, friendly, relaxed game.

Then I decided to put $50 on it. Just slapped a fifty right down on the table, and the girl who won got to keep the cash. And all heck broke loose.

Now, before we go any farther, I would like to again bring up the fact that there was no grape jelly for my biscuits. That really did spin me out. It is clear that my brain was not functioning properly at that moment.

Because what happened next was insanity. Harper and Mayah got these crazy-intense looks on their faces. I mean, I didn't know grade-school girls could even *look* like this. Foreheads all crinkled, sweat dripping down, biting their lips. Like these tiny little much cuter Jack Bauers trying to defuse a ticking bomb in *24*.

At first, me and Derek just figure they're into it, right? So we're cheering them on. Not trying to be jerks or anything, don't get me wrong. Just stuff like, "You got this, girls!" "See it through!" "No shame in losing! Even though the loser will be fifty bucks poorer!"

Then suddenly we realized . . . the girls weren't stressed because they wanted to *win* the money. No, they were actually *worried* they'd win

---

*I tried looking Grego up online, just to check its spelling, and the only thing I could find—no joke—was someone going, "What is Nate Bargatze talking about on his podcast with this game Grego! There's no such game!" So I guess we're the only ones who play it, and I can spell it however I want.

and deprive their cousin of the cash. They were such good friends they couldn't imagine beating each other.

All I could think was—this is life? And do gas stations carry grape jelly?

Harper and Mayah went back and forth, getting closer and closer to the winning score. And with each roll it got worse. Harper rolled a ten, and her knees started shaking. Mayah rolled a three and she breathed a huge sigh of relief.

None of us could believe what was going on. Me and Derek looked at each other like, "What do we do? Should the girls keep going? Should we tell them to quit?" Our wives looked at us like they were having serious second thoughts about their marriages. I was thinking, "It's a good thing Derek's the one who put money on the game and not me. Because that's totally what happened." Then my stomach grumbled.

Finally, Harper wins—and both girls burst into tears. Harper because she won, and Mayah because she feels bad that Harper feels so bad. Harper runs upstairs to her room and slams the door behind her, sobbing.

Our whole family sits there staring at each other. Finally my dad goes, "Well, to the victor goes the spoils." I still don't know if he was trying to be ironic.

Laura says, "Y'all are a bunch of idiots." Which she definitely did not mean with endearment.

My brother looks at me and says, "Maybe we should go talk to Mayah and Harper."

"Yeah," I say. "You're right."

Here's the thing about Derek. Sure, he can get under my skin, but that's what brothers do. We also look out for each other. Whenever we played football in the park—I'd always win, of course—if a bigger kid tried to push me around, my brother would always have my back. When I graduated high school and my brother was about to start his freshman year, I told people not to mess with him. He then proceeded to turn the drinking-fountain water into wine, so I guess I didn't have much to worry about.

And yeah, he's the second child, but he's also the middle child. So along with being annoyingly responsible, he's also the glue that holds our family together. Sometimes he makes trouble—always very calmly and coolly—but most of the time he's the one who fixes it. He's a good listener, he's sensitive, and he cares for people. Weirdest of all, he never tries to take credit for it. Even if he does take credit for games of Spades that he obviously lost.

So I follow Derek upstairs. We talk to our daughters—he does most of the talking—and he helps them realize that maybe the best thing to do is just split the money, fifty-fifty. Then my little brother smiles at me, and there's absolutely nothing irritating about it.

"You know what?" he says. "You're right. Dry biscuits really are the worst."

I look at him, size up the competition. "Play you in H-O-R-S-E at the next-door neighbor's hoop. Winner has to go find grape jelly."

"You're on."

BOWLING 101

The hardest class I took when I went to college was bowling. You probably think I'm not telling the truth, and you're right. The truth is all my classes were the hardest classes, which is why I failed all of them.

I went to Western Kentucky with one of my oldest friends from Old Hickory, P-P. Who got his nickname when a football hit . . . you know. Maybe I've explained it enough.

Out of all my friends, P is actually the smartest and most ambitious. I'm just gonna let that sit there for a second, all right? The most successful, real-job guy in my group is known, to this day, as P. At his current career, where he does "money stuff," to use an actual real term, even his boss knows him as P-P. That's because I told his boss that's what we call him, though I'm pretty sure it got him a raise or a "right on" or a Formula 409K or whatever it is people with real jobs try to get all the time.

College was a lot for me and P to take in. The year before, me and P had done a year of community college back home in Tennessee. We'd each lived with our parents, and "studying" was basically hanging out at my house watching *Jerry Springer* and eating frozen pizzas from the Piggly Wiggly, which were such delicious frozen pizzas. The closest thing we ever got to a super smart class like bowling was this one night, when our buddy Jeff rolled my dad's bowling ball down the stairs. About half-way down, I thought, "That was not a good idea." It left this big ol' dent in the wall. So I panicked for about thirty seconds, then I hung a poster over it and no one ever noticed.

Now that we were at Western Kentucky, not only were we taking *real* courses about *real* bowling, but me and P were living on our own for the very first time. We got to do what we wanted, go where we wanted, we even had to get furniture for our dorm room. Like, oh, I guess lamps do not grow naturally out of the floor like they do at my folks' house.

So our first week there, we went to find a coffee table at the local Goodwill. We pulled into the parking lot, and we saw a sign up outside for Employee of the Month. This dude had the most amazing name we'd ever heard in our lives.

Michael Loafmen.

That's right. Goodwill's hardest, most reliable worker. Michael. Loafmen.

We go, this Loafmen guy must really be something special. To earn an honor like that, with a name like that. This dude must be crushing it.

So me and P go inside and we find a guy who's working there, just a normal-looking guy who looks like any guy who'd work at a Goodwill—brown hair, better-than-me posture, a gleam in his eyes—and we ask him where the coffee tables are, and he goes "*Coffee tables?* What kind of place do you think this is! We don't have coffee tables! You people are ridiculous!"

Then we turn the corner, and right there is a stack of fifty coffee tables. Just a paradise of coffee tables. More coffee tables than any sane person could ever want in their life.

And me and P turn and look at each other, and we're like . . .

"Loafmen!"

We knew that was him. We just knew.

Was there any logical reason why? Heck no. In fact, it probably wasn't the real Michael Loafmen at all. But that was the whole point.

Our Michael Loafmen wasn't a real guy, he was a superhero. He made no sense. He was totally bad *and* perfectly good, all at the same time. He was the guy who somehow succeeded not despite being lazy—but because of it. Like, this dude was so unbelievably awful at his job that his boss could only stand back and go, "That Michael Loafmen! I wish I could fire him, but I respect his commitment to badness so much I think I'll promote him instead. Also, I love that name!"

Now, did we put even close to this much thought into it back then? Not at all. It just seemed kinda funny. But looking back, I am absolutely sure that I am still not putting much thought into it today. On that you have my guarantee.

After we got our coffee table—with literally *anti-help* from Michael Loafmen—me and P would drive by the Goodwill every now and then. And this dude was their Employee of the Month every single month after that. Seriously, for the entire year. I mean, sure, they probably just forgot to change the sign. But still—an impressive accomplishment for a Michael Loafmen.

He set a standard for lazy excellence that would've been hard for anyone to match. But I figured I'd give it a try in Bowling 101.

I happen to have a long history with bowling.

My dad's mom is actually in the Kentucky Bowling Hall of Fame. Do I know exactly what that means, to be in the Kentucky Bowling Hall of Fame? No, I don't. I have no idea what the process is. Maybe there's a vote, or some kind of bowling-themed raffle or bake-off. If I'm being honest, me and my grandmother weren't all that close. But she's definitely in that Hall of Fame somewhere, or at least that's what my dad tells me.

Then there was that dent that Jeff left in my parents' wall with my dad's bowling ball that one night when he rolled it down the stairs. As I said, I covered the bowling ball–shaped dent with a poster, and it may in fact be there to this day. I do not know.

So it's fair to say I have something of a legacy to live up to when it comes to bowling, which is why I took college bowling. Also, I thought it would be very easy. I mean, come on—bowling.

But from the beginning, I had a couple things working against my pursuit of greatness. First off, there was the time. That class was every Tuesday first thing in the morning, at 8 a.m.! Or maybe it was noon. I honestly can't remember. But either way, that's just crazy. Who bowls that early in the day? I am not bowling any time before 9 p.m. It's just not civilized.

As my one smart, responsible friend, P's main job at college was to make sure I got to class on time. He'd go, "I like to be five minutes early, not five minutes late." And I'd go, "Why show up at all?" So we'd have class, and I'd still be asleep, and he'd say, "Duuuude! Come on! We're gonna be late! Do it for Loafmen!"

Loafmen had become our thing, this call to arms for dumb college kids. If one of us was slacking off, we'd be like, "You are not Michael Loafmen material!"

Or, "You know who wouldn't be skipping class? Michael Loafmen!"

Or, "Get off your lazy butt, Loafmen!" Because we weren't exactly consistent with it. Which, of course, was classic Loafmen.

Tuesday mornings were extra hard, because every Monday night there was *Monday Night Raw*. This was peak WWF, before they changed it to an "E." We're talking Stone Cold Steve Austin, we're talking The Rock, we're talking Triple H. The best of the best. You'd hear their theme music, and they were electric, with the trash talk and the drama and who has the belt and who doesn't have the belt. And The Rock is kicking guys in the stomach and laying 'em out on the mat and hitting 'em with the People's Elbow. And we'd be going crazy in our room all night, wrestling and body slamming and whacking each other with aluminum pie pans, because they make this loud noise when you hit 'em. BAM! BAM! BAM!

And it was like—college wanted me to miss *this*? So I could wake up for bowling at 4 a.m.? Or noon or whatever?

Then morning would come around, and P would shout, "Come on, Loafmen! You got class in twenty minutes!" And I'd think about Michael Loafmen. I'd think about how no matter what, rain or shine, Michael Loafmen would make it to work every single day, just so he could give customers exactly the wrong information. And not even about complicated things, but about tables and whether or not they exist. And I'd drag myself out of bed, and I'd go to that bowling class.

Which is when I'd run into the other little problem. Because it turned out that Bowling 101 was actually really, really, I mean crazy hard.

The teacher was old and basically insane. On the first day of class, he started barking at us like a drill sergeant. "You think bowling is a game? You think bowling is fun? This is serious business! Bowling is war! You gotta fight!" It was like a weird, deleted bowling scene from *Full Metal Jacket* that was so bad they didn't even include it in the extended DVD.

I thought, well, at least we still get to bowl. The campus bowling alley was actually really nice. But Sgt. Slaughter never even let us pick up a bowling ball. The class was all theory. I didn't even know bowling *had* a theory! This dude wanted us to memorize the lanes and the dots and the arrows, plus all this mumbo jumbo about correct technique and form. Instead of bowling I should've just gone to med school. Then at least I'd be totally unqualified for something impressive.

The second class was all about calculating the score. A bunch of nonsense about strikes and bonus balls and doubling the frame with the square root of pie. I'm like, apple or pecan? Seriously, why are you teaching me this? We have computers to do this for us! That's how complicated scoring is in bowling. It's advanced math. This is probably why scientists invented computers in the first place. They were hanging out and bowling, nothing too competitive, just a friendly game, but, you know, still trying to keep score.

And they said, "I don't know how to do this. Do you know how to do this?"

"No idea."

"Welp, guess we should invent computers."

P could bug me as much as he wanted, but I bet I made it to three bowling classes all semester. Maybe four. I did show up for the final exam—and it was entirely on paper. No bowling involved. P-P got a C—a C!—and he was truly a good bowler. I failed the exam. And the class. And every other class. My parents said, "We are not going to keep paying for this. There are much cheaper ways to get gutter balls." So that was it for me and college. (For the record: I did one year of community college, all remedial classes. Then one semester at Western Kentucky, failed everything. Total credits? Zero.)

After I flunked out, me and P went to the campus bowling alley one last time, so for once I could actually, you know, bowl. And for the very first time, we stopped and looked at the plaque that listed the top all-time scores at Western Kentucky.

No joke—right there, right next to a perfect 300 game, was the name "M. Loafmen."

Sure, I guess that could've been Martin Loafmen. Or Max or Mary or whatever. But deep down in my soul, I knew—I just knew—that that was Michael Loafmen. *Our* Michael Loafmen. And I knew that somehow he achieved that perfect game in the most ridiculous way that he didn't even earn. Like blindfolded, or maybe accidentally, while he was playing golf.

Legend.

A few years later, after P had graduated and started his career in, like, money or whatever, while I was working at Applebee's not making any money at all, we got back into bowling. And by "got back into it," I mean we were obsessed.

Every Thursday night, we'd go to Quartermania at Hermitage Lanes. On that night and that night only, everything cost a quarter. There were quarter games. Quarter drinks. Quarter food. We'd get there after 9 p.m., because we aren't a bunch of animals, and we'd close the place out. Just bowling and dropping quarters like a couple millionaires all night long.

I had one goal, and one goal only. I wanted to redeem myself. To finally live up to the standards set by one Michael Loafmen. Though if I'm being honest, mostly I just loved how cheap those games were. I mean, we could bowl forever and not pay more than a couple bucks—that's just crazy. But the Loafmen thing felt right when I said it, so I'm sticking with it.

I can't explain exactly why, but to this day, Michael Loafmen—a dude I probably have never met, and if I did it was only long enough to learn he might not know what a coffee table is—remains a huge part of my life. Whenever I need a fake name for anything, I always use Michael Loafmen. My email is Michael.Loafmen. When I get pizza delivered, it's for Michael Loafmen. When I stay at a hotel, I check in as Michael Loafmen.* My comedian friend Julian McCullough even got me a fake Michael Loafmen ID. One time I went to get the key to my hotel room, and the lady at the front desk wouldn't accept my real ID with my real name on it, so I pulled the fake one out of my wallet and said, "How about this fake ID with my fake name on it?" She goes, "That works."

Which is essentially like if I'm 19 and a store won't let me buy alcohol with my real ID, so I go, "Hold on, I have another ID that says I'm 21," and they say, "Great. Drink up."

In the same way that Bruce Wayne is Batman, I want Michael Loafmen to be my alter ego. So I was determined to bowl a 300. I wanted that perfect game at Quartermania. I wanted it so bad.

Me and P played so much, we got to know the quirks of each of the lanes at Hermitage. They all had their own personalities. They each had their own tiny warps and bends. We didn't need to worry about any theory. We didn't need to read anything about the lines and the arrows and the placement of the pins. We definitely didn't care about technique. We just felt that bowling in our guts. Most of all, we had fun.

---

*Note to self: Change both OldBlue password and Michael Loafmen email and hotel check-in. The pizza ordering can probably stay.

We made up all these jokes that were only funny to us. If our ball squeezed between a bunch of easy pins it should've hit, we'd shout, "It ran through a forest with tight trees!" If we got a strike, we'd pretend to pick up a phone out of thin air and shout, "Hold the line!" If we almost guttered, we'd wipe our brows and shout, "Whew!"

I even had a lucky ball that Laura, who was only my girlfriend at the time, gave me. It looked like the psycho killer from *Scream*. You know, that weird, creepy mask with the big open mouth. So yeah. Totally lucky.

And it was working. I was getting better and better. Closer and closer to that mythical 300. Then finally I had one game where everything seemed to click. I bowled a 9, then a spare, then I struck out all the rest. I sat down at our little table with a pencil and paper and a calculator to figure out the score, then I remembered that this was real life, and we were normal, sane human beings, so I looked at the computer instead.

I had bowled a 269.

Well, guess what? In the very next game, I bowled another few strikes right off the bat. In the very next game! So when you think about it, technically I did bowl a 300. Sure, it was broken up over two games. But still, a 300.

P has told me that I do not understand the meaning of the word "technically." And I'm like, "Everyone calls you P." And he goes, "Yeah, but I'm still the smart one. And you still flunked bowling." All I can say is, "Sad but true."

No matter what P-P says, I believe Michael Loafmen, if such a man even exists, would respect my perfect game. Precisely because it's so blatantly not perfect. He'd be a little embarrassed that I failed college bowling, but he'd be proud that I failed it so spectacularly. As for flunking out altogether, my guess is he'd shrug and order me a random pizza under his name.

Am I saying that after all these years I'm finally Michael Loafmen material? Let's not get crazy.

But it's always important to have goals.

RANDOM FOOD THING 2: I HATE ONIONS

I hate onions.

I don't want onions on Big Macs. I don't want onions on pizza. I don't want onions on top of other onions that you just happen to buy because you are a psycho who loves onions. I hate onions in any form. And be careful—because restaurants will try to trick you into eating onions, even if that's the last thing on earth you want to eat. They're sneaky, those guys.

Now they're adding chives to stuff, and they're not even telling you your food's got onions in it. They go, "Trust us! It's a garnish! It's flavorless! It's just a nice little splash of green in your mashed potatoes, like parsley or something!" But chives do not taste like parsley. They do not taste like nothing. You know what they taste like?

They taste like onions.

Because chives. Are. Onions.

There was this time, about fifteen years ago, when chives were banned everywhere because some chives from a company in New York got contaminated with listeria. Seriously. This is a real thing. It happened, and it was one of my favorite times in this country. I mean, I have no idea what listeria is—I am pretty sure it's a mouthwash or something—but if it wants to take out the world's chives supply, I am all for this particular form of badness.

I was so happy during this chives ban. So happy. And honestly, I got kind of lazy, because I no longer had to tell my waiter in advance that I did not want chives on or next to or even within half a mile of my meal.

Then all of a sudden, chives were back. And I was out of practice. I wasn't telling them no chives, and they were putting those bad boys on everything like they held a grudge. "Hey, it's that Nate Bargatze—you know, the one who hates chives! Now's our chance to get him good!" French fries, drinking water, chocolate cake—you name it, they put chives on it. No mercy.

So that's why today, for the record, I am telling you, I am telling waiters, I am telling cooks, I am telling the whole world—I do not care how hungry I get, or how desperate for food I am, I will not eat your onions. I don't care what they look like, how you cook them, or what you call them. Because I. Hate. Onions.

Except for onion rings. Those I can do. You know, basically anything deep-fried.

KISS THE GIRL

Me and my wife Laura get into fights about music mostly because she is normal and I am not.

Normal people, like in this case Laura I guess, really love music. It means something to them. For whatever reason, it's a big part of their lives. When we go on a family road trip, Laura puts together an entire playlist for that specific journey.

I don't mean it's just a collection of songs. That would be way too easy. I mean that there is a very exact order so that each song has a very precise purpose for every part of the trip. Like, "Oh, we'll be driving right past that beautiful meadow then, here's a light and inspirational song that's perfect for that moment." Or, "Pretty sure that's when we stop at that truck-stop McDonald's to use the bathroom. Let's go with heavy metal."

Then she'll ask me what kind of special, meaningful songs I want for this epic journey we're about to go on, and I'll go, "I don't know . . . something with guitars? Or maybe a flute? That's an instrument, right?"

I do listen to music. I do. It just doesn't mean anything to me.

I mean seriously, I hear music the way a dog does. The words could be anything. Every song I hear is "bark bark bark woof woof woof!" and I just smile, stick my head out the car window, and let the wind blow through my hair.

I'd say I take in music the way plants do, except that's actually giving me too much credit, because I'm pretty sure I read some article that said that plants actually grow better to happy, upbeat music. You could give me the darkest, most depressing song in the world, literally it could be about men marching off to war, and I could sing it for you with all the joy and happiness of a new Taylor Swift hit, that's how little music means to me.

And yes, the only reason I know who Taylor Swift is is because my wife refuses to allow me to be a complete outcast from normal society. Every singer I know about is the biggest American singer on the planet Earth. You will never hear me say a band where you will be like, "Who is that? You must really have your finger on the pulse of indie rock or jazz or something else that the most average dumb American would never listen to." I'm the guy who goes, "Hey, have you heard about this dude who's really shaking things up? Name is Ulvis. I guess the girls really dig him or something." And if there is some weird indie singer out there who is actually named Ulvis, just remember I was first on board.

It's a good thing that Laura is one of the people who actually does care about music, though. First off, someone's gotta keep watch over our daughter, because Harper could be listening to something completely inappropriate about drugs or Satan or boys, and I'd be like, "Hey, that's a catchy tune."

And second, because a song is why me and Laura got together in the first place. Though honestly, even after all these years I'm still not exactly sure what it's about.

Things didn't start out so great when I first met Laura.

Of course, I pretty much fell in love with her the first time I laid eyes on her. As for her, I'm pretty sure she thought I was dumb. That's because she always goes out of her way to tell people, "I thought Nate was dumb."

I met Laura on my second day as a host at Applebee's. I was twenty years old, broke, and I'd barely even had a real job before. I had no idea what I was doing with my life. If someone had said, "What is your goal five years from now?" I would've looked at them and been like, "Well, tomorrow they're teaching me how to seat people. At tables. So that's neat." Because that's all a host at a restaurant does. You just need to know how to walk people to an empty table, and maybe also wear pants that day. I could handle both of those things, like 80 percent of the time, so they went, "Why not? Give this kid a job."

My body was really skinny, but I had this round baby face and those big doe eyes that I named this book after, so that was helpful in a professional place of work. I balanced it out by doing sophisticated things like wearing a rubber band around my wrist. I'm not sure how that started—I think I saw a basketball player wearing one once. Honestly,

Rubber band. So cool.

he probably did it on accident. Saw it on his wrist at the end of the day and went, "A rubber band? That's just stupid." Meanwhile, I bought a whole box from Staples and wore one nonstop for the next six years, like, "Now I'm an athlete too!"

I had a buzz cut. Laura says I had long hair that was dyed to look like a giraffe. I say that if I did ever dye my hair like that, it is because everyone knows that giraffes are the coolest animals at the zoo except elephants, who basically have buzz cuts. So, you know, touche, or whatever. Anyway, this is an actual ongoing debate about my actual own head to this day, and I will probably lose.

Laura, on the other hand, was this woman of the world. Or at least Alabama, which is where she was from. She was the big dog of the waitresses, and she was a couple years older than me, which, when you're only twenty, is like, "Wow. That's some life experience there." I mean, this is someone who grew up watching *Dallas* and *Falcon Crest* on TV! She had a boyfriend, which I tried to forget, and she knew the whole menu, which I never even bothered to remember. I was obsessed with the movie *Office Space*, where Jennifer Aniston plays a waitress, so I'd see Laura in that Applebee's apron and think, "*Yes*. She is Jennifer Aniston. I am in love."

Then she told me she'd moved close to Nashville to take college classes and try to get into the music business, and I might as well have been listening to Ulvis. College? The music business? Those words meant nothing to me. It was just "bark bark bark woof woof woof!" and *how the heck was I gonna impress this woman?*

To be fair, it's not like I had much experience. I'd barely ever been on a date before.

Back in high school, I got asked by a girl I knew from church to go to another school's prom. She was a year older than me, and I thought, "Sure, how hard can this romance stuff be?" Before the dance, we went to a steakhouse for dinner with a few other people, and the dude sitting next to me leaned over and said, "Hey, the guys are just gonna split the bill between us."

Suddenly I realized that I was supposed to pay for my date, and I had maybe $2 in my pocket. *Okay, I guess romance is very, very hard after all.*

So everyone else ordered these big, thick juicy steaks. Rib eyes, strip steaks, T-bones, filet mignons. Whatever cut of meat there was to eat, these people ordered it. And I'm like, "I will have the water, please."

My date is cutting into her beef, just chowing down and digging into all the sides, the broccoli, the mac 'n' cheese, the mashed potatoes— which I'm all for, by the way, I love a woman with a healthy appetite—but I am sitting there starving and terrified, and it is not a good combination. I'm practically drooling all over this tablecloth, and each time she orders a new dish I'm going, "But have you tried the water? It really is very good. An excellent vintage, I believe. I've heard they're adding this new ingredient called fluoride."

I ended up gnawing on my own fist for the rest of the night, owing these other guys a hundred bucks. They all went on to marry their dates. I'd get these fancy invitations in the mail that were like, "We'd invite you to our wedding, but you still owe us from that steak dinner." My date pretty much never spoke to me again.

So when I started working at Applebee's and I saw this beautiful Jennifer Aniston waitress who was totally out of my league, I thought, "I gotta do the exact opposite. I am going to be myself, without apology, no matter what."

I might as well have gone "bark bark bark woof woof woof!"

I had just started my shift one day when I looked up at the TV.

What the heck was this garbage? It was a couple boring dudes just sitting around in dusty gray suits, and they were talking and talking, who knows what about, and around them were all these random charts and graphics and numbers. Like, I thought this was an Applebee's, not Ruth Chris!

So naturally I walked with great purpose and stamina over to the bar and grabbed the remote. Then I stopped. I was still the new guy, and I'm pretty much just naturally slow, but even I knew that there are certain rules when it comes to the remote control at a restaurant.

If you think deciding who gets to control the remote is tough in your living room, you ain't seen nothing till you been to an Applebee's. It's some kind of restaurant *Game of Thrones.* You got the manager, who's supposedly the TV King, but he's always being conspired against by the Duke of Bartending or the Queen's In-Laws Waiting Tables. Like, "The King just went to use the bathroom! Change it to the Hallmark Channel, then hide the remote under the bread basket! Stick that knife in deep and give it a good ol' twist!"

Me—I was barely even the Court Jester at this point. I had no rights to anything. But what kind of thinking was that? I needed to make my mark here! I had to impress people! After all, I wore a rubber band around my wrist. I was practically in the NBA!

So I grabbed the remote off the bar, and I clicked the TV over to golf—which honestly is where all Applebee's TVs rightfully belong. Then I felt a tap on my shoulder.

It was Laura. Her face was flushed kind of red, which probably wasn't a good sign, but somehow made her look even more like Jennifer Aniston.

"Excuse me," she said. "Did you just change my TV?"

I looked down at the remote in my hand. "Um, yeah," I said.

"And why, might I ask, did you do that?"

I frowned. *Come on, Nate—show her how good you are at thinking on your feet!*

"Well, that last channel, it just kept showing these numbers scrolling across the bottom, over and over. Like this big mess of stuff."

Yes! Nailed it.

"Oh," she said. "Do you think it was the *stock market* maybe?"

Or not.

"Well," I said, "I don't know *what* it is."

Then I turned around and walked away. Like, *That'll show her!*

Maybe, just maybe, that's where Laura's whole "I thought Nate was dumb" thing comes from. But who knows? If I'm honest, there are so many examples to choose from.

A while later, a bunch of us from work all decided to go out.

We piled into my car, which at the time was this giant, champagne-colored Buick.* It was this big boat of a car, one of those things that maybe your great-grandpa drove around and thought it was a real fine vehicle. I called it the Real Car's Car.

I named him after this pro wrestler, William Regal, the Real Man's Man. He was this big dude with flowing blond hair and when he entered the ring he had this catchy theme song that went, "He's a man! Such a man! He's a real, real man's man." Honestly, how could I not name my car after such an awesome winner?

Laura was one of the people tagging along that night. By this point, the situation with her wasn't exactly looking great for me. I mean, she was always polite enough, I guess. But just in the way that fellow employees are usually polite to each other. We knew some of the same people, we went to some of the same parties. But Laura would always find ways to drop how cute her boyfriend was, which was super annoying. And then there was the whole thing about me being dumb. So, you know, not ideal.

But being dumb had its advantages. Sure, I was the kind of guy who had no problem naming his car after a pro wrestler. But . . . I was also the kind of guy who had *no problem* naming his car after a pro wrestler. I'd been a total idiot in front of Laura a bunch of times. But that wasn't gonna stop me. I wasn't embarrassed. I wasn't gonna say I'm sorry. I was just gonna do it more, and even bigger than before.

---

*To anyone who is actually paying attention to what I'm writing, this car was about two or three generations after Old Blue, who by now was down in Texas enjoying his retirement. He may have been gone, but the spirit of nicknaming every vehicle I ever drove was going strong.

Was this some kind of strategy I actually thought up to win her over? Heck no. I needed spellcheck just to write "strategy." I could've sworn there used to be a "d" in there. But that's the thing about being dumb—I had no choice. I was too dumb to be anything else. I just had to own who I was and hope it all worked out.

So we were all driving in the Real Car's Car to wherever it was we were going, and everyone was laughing and hollering, and Laura was in the back talking with someone else, probably about how awesome her boyfriend was. I was getting lost in all the noise, trying to figure out some way, any way, to get her to notice me. Some way to stand out. Some way to break through the racket and be perfectly, ridiculously, dumb ol' me. And then it hit me.

I reached into the glove compartment and pulled out one of the only CDs I owned—the soundtrack to *The Little Mermaid*.

Because it just so happened that there was one kind of music I actually knew the words to. One kind of music that sounded like more than a dog barking or a plant growing or whatever. One kind of music that meant something. It was Disney music.

Part of it was because Disney music is awesome. I mean, these tunes are for everyone, and the words are simple enough that someone with a brain like mine can understand them. But part of it was because for me, this music was personal. As you may or may not remember, my kid sister Abigail was ten years younger than me, and she was one of my favorite people in the world. She looked up to me—probably because I was taller than her, but whatever, she did—and whenever I drove her around, we'd always listen to Disney music. *Beauty and the Beast* and *Lion King* and *Aladdin* and *Hercules*. All the good stuff. Just blasting it—belting out the words, forgetting about life, and having a good time. Just being ourselves. Until the words truly meant something, even to someone like me.

So I popped in my CD, and I shushed everyone in the car. And you know what? They actually shushed. Honestly, I think even they were shocked by what was going on. How often does a dude in his twenties tell you to shut up so he can play Disney tunes?

Then I started playing my favorite song of all, "Kiss the Girl." Or, you know, whatever the one is by the lobster or whatever.

I turned that thing all the way up, and I wasn't just listening, I wasn't just singing along—I was booming out those words, just like I did with Abigail. And sure, I probably made up a few of the lyrics, a couple "bark bark woof woofs" here and there. But I got most of them right. I was belting out this song at the top of my lungs for the whole world to hear. And for one person especially.

I turned my head and I caught Laura out of the corner of my eye, and she had this big ol' smile on her face. She was so incredibly beautiful, like even Jennifer Aniston in *Office Space* couldn't hold a candle to her. She looked in my eyes, I looked in hers, I sang something about a fish, and I just knew. I felt it. I really did.

Anyway, a few days went by.

One night we were closing up the restaurant. Just the two of us, getting everything back in order, sweeping up, the TV totally turned off. I looked over at Laura, and out of nowhere she threw her leg over her broom, kickstarted it, and pretended to ride it like a witch. Of course, she now says she meant it to be a horse, not a witch's broomstick, and this is an actual ongoing debate we will have that I will probably lose.

Then she looked at me and made this clicking noise with her mouth. *Click click click.* Like, come on—here we go!

That was it. She was beautiful, she was funny, and she'd just invited me on our very first road trip together. Sure, it was on a broom—a *broom*, not a horse, or a giraffe, or an elephant—but I loved how weird it was. She owned it, just like I did.

And knowing her, she had the playlist all picked out.

GET YOUR HEAD ABOVE WATER

HELP WANTED: MUST LOVE SNACKS

When I finished high school and realized college wasn't going to work out, I knew I was gonna do one kind of job for the rest of my life.

The kind where the title of the job is exactly what you do in that job.

Jobs like firefighter, pro wrestler, rock star. Simple, straightforward, uncomplicated jobs. I mean, someone had to do them, right? Why not me? Which is how I became a water meter reader.

And you know what? A simple job is not a bad thing. A guy in my neighborhood told me he was an information systems auditor, and I said, "Oh, so you audit the information that the system gives you." To be honest, I don't even know what it means to audit something. I talked to him about it for a few minutes, and I don't think he does either.

But that is not a problem with reading water meters. When I tell you that I was a water meter reader, there is no mystery about what I did. I went from one water meter to another, and I read them. That's it. I have nothing more to tell you about that. There was no special technique, there were no surprises. There was no "Well, sometimes I had to read *to* the water meters to help them fall asleep at night." Nope. I would wake up every morning, I would go get the company truck, and I would drive through West Wilson County, Tennessee, reading water meters. That's what I did and that's who I was.

The other great thing about those kinds of jobs is that you really end up being your own boss. Reading water meters was so fast and easy that I usually finished my work around noon. Then I became a real self-starter. I would drive my company truck over the county line, out of West Wilson's jurisdiction, and go to my friend P-P's house, where P was still living at home. As you might remember, we went to college together. They gave him a diploma and they asked me to leave.

Oh, and I have now explained my friend's nickname a couple times, but it bears repeating that he got it because a football once hit him in the shoulder. No, it didn't. Just making sure you're listening.

Anyway, when I arrived at P's house, do not think that I just slacked off. No, I worked hard to avoid responsibility. I had to drive the company truck *all the way* behind his house to make sure no one could see it. Then I had to lug the (slightly) heavy yellow utility light off the roof and put it in the back, just to be safe. Then I had to drag over the trash can to hide the license plate. Sometimes I'd tweak my thumb. Maybe even break a sweat. And if that doesn't sound like ambition to you, I don't know what more to say.

Then I would take a nap. I mean right there, in the truck, I would literally just lie back, cover my eyes with my hat, and sleep for the rest of the day. Or, if I was feeling extra, extra motivated, I would go into P's house, grab a snack, watch his family's TV, and take a nap there. In case you're curious, P himself was out, busy at his accounting job, where they actually expected him to, like, be there.

But I don't want you to think I was some kind of freeloader, mooching off my buddy. As my own boss, I understood what it meant to be responsible. So sometimes I would also help P's mom with her own small business. She sold these little prayer books called devotionals out of her house. Devotionals have sayings on each page that can be as simple as "Choose faith over fear" or "Visualize God's love, purity, and guidance" or my personal favorite "Diet Coke is a breakfast beverage." Her company was called Inspiration Celebration.

I am a man who is not qualified to inspire or to celebrate, but for some strange reason this lovely lady thought I should answer her business's phones. My sales pitch to potential customers who called in went something like:

"Hello."

Or on occasion: "Hey there."

And once I think I managed to say, "Hello. Celebration Inspiration. Oh. Um. Wait. I mean Inspiration Celebration. Or . . . Anyway. Never mind."

Thinking back, I'm pretty sure I made the callers feel so depressed that they needed to buy devotionals just to go on with their day. So kind of genius actually. I sold four of them. Never even asked for commission.

Being at West Wilson County Utilities was great. I read water meters and I slept, snacked, and watched TV.* And I got paid for it. I even had a 401(k), which to this day I do not know what that is. My job was simple, it was easy, and I got to be my own boss.

So I figured I might just read water meters for the rest of my life. I mean, why not?

Before the utility company, I had tried a few other jobs that started out simple but ended up being way too complex.

For a while, I delivered pizzas, which are exactly what you think they are. They are pizzas. And if you decide to be your own boss by watching TV and taking a nap, they are cold pizzas. Then you have to find a different job.

I also tried recycling tires. I guess that one needs explaining. Basically, there was a big nationwide recall of car tires, so I helped my buddy collect and ship them for reprocessing. But that's just fancy talk for

---

*To West Wilson Utilities: I am positive that no employee does that now or has ever done that except for me. I came up with the idea on my own. Like I said: self-starter.

"I tossed giant rubber donuts into the back of a truck." At the end of the day, I'd go to Laura's place filthy, and I'd wash off using her soft, snow-white bath towels, which ended up looking like an old barbecue grill. She would ask why I wrecked her nice clean towels, and I would shout, "Showing initiative!" But she didn't appreciate my ambition.

Then there was drunk driving, which was not something I did, but it was my job. You know, not in a bad way. Well, not *too* bad.

Me and the couple who owned the drunk-driving car.
I can't believe the high school kids didn't think I was cool.

My dad knew a married couple who owned one of those special cars that uses a computer to simulate what it's like to drive drunk. So they'd go to high schools and they'd put a kid behind the wheel, they'd push a button and go, "Hey, you teenage idiot—you like to drink beer? All right, drive across that parking lot and don't knock over any of those cones."

Then the kid would hit the gas, the computerized car would go crazy, and they'd hit every cone, like, "Yeah, that was you driving drunk and you just killed a bunch of old people walking their puppies, which is why you are a teenage idiot."

So my job was to drive along the East Coast with this couple, going from school to school, helping to maintain this incredibly special car, which was a Dodge Neon but should've been an actual special car like a Camaro. At each school, while the owners were preaching about the evils of drinking and driving, I got to set up the cones. I also got to set up the Dodge Neon, which should've been a Camaro, by putting the kids' weights and a fake blood alcohol level into the car's computer. Then I'd push a button, and just like that they'd drive drunk.

But this was a crazy adventure for me. I was still a kid myself. I mean, I wasn't even old enough to drink the stuff this drunk-car was warning everyone about. And all of a sudden I was making money and staying in cheap hotels. I was traveling for the first time in my life to New York and Florida, and all these pretty high school girls would say, "Wow, is this alcoholic car yours? How does it work?"

Then they'd get into my shiny car and I'd smile my goofy smile and smooth back my hair, which was pretty much just a buzz cut, and I would say something real charming like:

"Hello."

Or on occasion: "Hey there."

Then I'd ask them how much they weighed. Because the computer needed to know. They'd get all angry and huffy because I guess asking a cute teenage girl her weight is not something one should do. But hey, it was 2000 and 9/11 was just around the corner, so didn't we really have other things to worry about?

One night the special car that I was responsible for was stolen. Where was I when this happened? Was I maybe blowing my per diem at the vending machines? Who's to really say. It's possible that something was recorded in the police report, but please don't bother investigating.

We found the car the next day, abandoned on the side of the road. Not a scratch on it. In my defense, if anything the thieves probably learned a valuable lesson. Like, "We could've sworn we were sober when we went on that joyride! Where did all those crazy cones appear from?! We'll never enter our weight into a computer again!"

That was the end of that job. Without even realizing it, I had saved up almost $10,000—not necessarily because the pay was amazing, but because on the road with the company I had never paid for a thing. It was great, because it was the most money I'd ever had, and awful, because it was the most money I'd ever had. I forgot about seeing the country, went home, and spent it all on Diet Coke and bags of Doritos.

But I did figure one thing out.

My next job would be straightforward. It would be uncomplicated. And I would have all the time in the world to do important stuff, like watch TV, take naps, and, I guess, sell devotionals.

Water meters, here I come.

I pretty much thought I'd found the perfect job. If I'm being honest, I would probably be reading meters and losing customers for P's mom to this day if the county utility company didn't finally try to make me, you know, *not* read water meters.

Which I obviously wasn't qualified for.

It was right after the time of 9/11—yes, I told you it was around the corner—when the entire country was coming together in a spirit of unity in the face of evil and adversity. And I was very cool with that. I'm a big fan of spirits of unity, and I do not enjoy evil or adversity.

We were all chipping in. Everyone was supposed to be on guard against the terrorists. No one knew where they might strike next. And that apparently included the water and power plant in West Wilson County, Tennessee.

We had a manager named Trey, and he was such a cool guy. He was a couple years older than me, and a couple inches taller. He had a chinstrap beard, and most importantly he got to take his company truck home at night and drive it whenever he wanted, possibly because he was not taking hidden secret naps on the job, but who really knows.

Me, Trey, and the company truck. He was a wise man.

Trey and the utility bigwigs said, "Hey, we got a patriotic duty here. Maybe they got the Twin Towers, maybe they attacked the Pentagon, but there is no way they're gonna get near West Wilson County utilities." So in the dead of night, all us workers were recruited to stand watch over this water tower surrounded by acres of grass and trees and fields and possibly some very suspicious squirrels I'm sure were up to no good.

We were ready for anything, armed to the teeth—by which I mean we had teeth. We also may have had some clipboards and some pens, which I'm sure would've come in handy if the terrorists had evil meters that needed to be read. So all throughout the night, whenever anyone suspicious approached, I would puff up my chest, hold my clipboard at the ready, and confidently announce:

"Hello."

Or on occasion: "Hey there."

Then I would realize it was just another dude who worked for the county, because honestly who else would be out in rural Tennessee at the water company in the middle of a humid September night? Either that, or the terrorists got one look at me from a mile away and said, "They got *this* dude guarding this place? I think we can cross target number five off our list. Clearly someone back at the terrorist office headquarters made a mistake, because this is obviously not a high priority for the Americans."

National security was not the right job for me. My manager Trey, being a cool guy and even cooler manager, maybe noticed this. Because a little while later, I was catching a ride to work in his company truck, and the two of us were listening to *The Bob & Tom Show*. It featured important guests like Floyd the Truck Driver and Captain Dave of the Chum Dumpster and had sophisticated humor.

So I kind of mentioned, just offhand, that I'd always wanted to try stand-up comedy myself. And yeah, I had always admired Jerry Seinfeld, who made this neat little TV show that my family loved. Called *Seinfeld*. And I had written in my high school yearbook that someday I wanted to perform at Zanies, which was Nashville's only real comedy club.

But I also said I wanted to play basketball in the NBA. Both goals seemed about as realistic. (Side note: As you know, I did play basketball in the Nashville Baptist Association. So technically I have accomplished all my goals.)

Now, the thing about Trey is that he was a lot more than his company truck. He was married and he had a ton of kids and it just kind of seemed like he'd figured it all out. He had a sort of wisdom about him. This knack for figuring out what you really wanted—even if that meant leaving the safe world of meter reading—and telling you what you needed to hear.

So when I said I'd thought about giving stand-up a try, Trey got this gleam in his eye, and he said all excited, "Hey dude, you gotta do that stand-up thing!" Then he told me that Michael Clay, a guy I'd seen around who also worked at the utility company, was thinking of moving to Chicago to take some improv classes at Second City. I should go with him and give stand-up a try.

It's not so much that Trey thought there was anything wrong with reading water meters—he works there to this day, and he's still a good friend of mine—it's more that he sensed that I wanted to do something different. He could've been like, "Son, I know about the naps. You ain't meant for much in this world." But instead he said, "Comedy? Well, you can't be any worse at it than reading water meters." Come to think of it, there is a chance he was also thinking of what was best for the water company.

Somehow, everything Trey said just made sense. Did I know squat about Chicago? Heck no. I'd barely ever left Tennessee. Did I have a clue how to break into stand-up? I'd never even tried an open mic at Zanies. Did I really even know Michael Clay? Well, I knew he was a huge Vanderbilt football fan like me, so at least he could embrace long shots.

So I had pretty much jack squat. But I did have a place to start. I had a sense of purpose. And I had a job with a pretty simple title. You stand. You're up. And you, like, comedied or something.

Maybe I could figure that last part out.

I WOULD LEAVE A NOTE

I found out the whole world wasn't all Christian the first time I moved away from the South. It was very surprising, because no one had informed me of this fact before I left Tennessee.

I was barely over twenty, and I had just moved to Chicago with my buddy Michael Clay. As you may recall, because I literally just talked about this in the last chapter, he was really only a dude I'd seen around town every now and then. But we did have a mutual friend named Trey, so naturally we said, "Hey, let's make this major life transition together."

Michael Clay—I always call him by his whole name to this day, and no one including me knows why—had never been to Chicago before in his life. I'd maybe been there once as a child, though I've talked to my family about this and none of us can remember. Michael Clay does look like Richard Kimble in the *Fugitive* when he's on the run there, so maybe that's it.

Anyway, Michael Clay wanted to take an improv class at Second City, and I wanted to learn how to be a comic, like Seinfeld, because he was my favorite comedian. But the two of us had no idea what we were doing. About, like, anything.

The other big problem was that no one could understand a word we said. Shortly after we got there, Michael Clay met this cute girl who was kinda tall and had this punk style that he'd only ever seen on TV. She said to him, "I'd love to have a conversation or something, but you sound like a banjo. All I can hear is *Twong! Ba-ding, ba-ding, ba-ding-ding-ding!*"

He tried to argue with her, but when he opened his mouth the only thing that came out was "Foggy Mountain Breakdown."

But honestly I wasn't much better than Michael Clay. I could always tell when someone didn't understand what he said. Probably because they'd go, "Huh?" So I'd helpfully repeat it for him. And then they would tell me, "I don't know what you said either." Then we would write it down.

We were also different because we were both Christian. Even though I am not always the best Christian, like my parents want me to be. They became born-again Christian right after I was born, which meant I had them when they were most Christian. I mean Eighties and Nineties Christian, which is basically as Christian as you can get. I thought "s*cks" was a swear word. But in small-town Tennessee, where I grew up, even if you weren't the most Christian, you were still very, very Christian.

Michael Clay was about as Christian as me, and he actually had a glass jar in his room where he kept his "tithing money." This is literally 10 percent of your income that you set aside for your local church. He barely had an income, and he didn't even have a local church in Chicago. I'm pretty sure we only went to church when we went back to Tennessee, just to check in with God. As if He wasn't watching us up north.

But Michael Clay would be like, "Well, if I find a buck on the ground, I can toss a dime in the jar. I'm sure there's a preacher somewhere who needs it." Eventually he just gave all $118 to St. Jude's Children's Hospital. As I said, he barely had an income.

Back home, church wasn't just a thing you went to, it was who you were. If you met someone you didn't know, you wouldn't say, "Nice to meet you" or even, "What's your name?" You'd say, "What church do you go to?" But it turned out that the people I met in Chicago were a little less . . . devout. Once I was talking to this guy and I honestly don't remember how religion even came up. Out of habit I was probably like, "Hey, what church do you go to?" Or "Hey, that Jesus—pretty cool, right?" Whatever it was, this dude looked at me and goes, "Wait, you're Christian? So you believe in God?"

And I go, "Wait, you don't?"

I mean, the not-Christian thing was shocking enough. But to not even believe in God? At all? That was crazy. I'd never met anybody who didn't believe in God before. Don't get me wrong, I wasn't there to judge. God would do that to that poor soul. I actually hesitated getting to know the dude too well, because once we died I knew I'd never see him again. Sorry, that's enough jokes. In all honesty, though, he was a wonderful guy, and I still talk to him to this day. As I still pray for him to this day.

Me and Michael Clay tried to make the best of our new life. We found this tiny apartment to rent in this pretty central area called Bucktown. Back then our place was maybe a few hundred bucks a month, and we could barely afford that. Now that I'm older and it's a much more expensive neighborhood, I'm like, "We should've bought that place!" Then I remember I was twenty and I could barely afford to buy a pizza. Our apartment was in a basement. It was small, dark, and kind of a dump, and we could hear this suspicious scratching sound behind the walls, but we loved the place anyway because young people are so stupid.

But then, right after we moved in, Chicago got hit by a heat wave. Now, that was no big deal to us. We were from the South, we were used to heat and humidity. We were also both fans of Vanderbilt football, so we were used to pain. But we were also used to air-conditioning. Every building in Tennessee has central air. No one likes hot pain, not even Vandy fans.

Our basement apartment. I mean, we were basically locals.

So we went to switch on the air in our tiny basement apartment, and there wasn't any. I don't mean it was broken or the switch wasn't working or something. I mean it just didn't, like, exist. At all. It made no sense! It was ninety-five degrees down there! We called up the landlady, and she said, "Nope, no air. You gotta buy your own unit for the window."

At this point, we needed oxygen, we honestly couldn't breathe, so me and Michael Clay went outside to sit on the stoop. We said, "What is going on up in this part of the world? Buy your own air conditioner? How do you even do that? It's lawless here!"

Speaking of which. Right while we're sitting there, this car that's parallel parked in front of us pulls out. And the guy in it bumps the car in front of him *and* the car behind him. And he takes off.

Our jaws dropped.

I mean, this dude barely even tapped these cars, but back home—you just wouldn't do that. If you dinged a door, you'd say, "Oh my gosh, I need to find these people and be a good neighbor!" If you couldn't, you'd just sleep next to the car until they got back. Or at the very least you'd leave a note with your contact information and Social Security number.

But this guy—he just leaves! Like it's nothing!

So we were seriously like, "Do we do something? Do we need to report this to the police? Should we find the owners of these two bumped cars, then arm ourselves and patrol the streets?" And so I did the only thing that made sense. The only thing that any rational, red-blooded, law-abiding American would do.

I got out a piece of paper, and I wrote down this scofflaw's license plate number. I really did. If the people of Chicago, who didn't believe in air-conditioning, would not stand up for what's right, then I would do it for them.

Of course, I never actually did anything with the license plate number. Probably left the paper in my pocket and ran it through the wash, which I do all the time and which is very annoying, because it gets lint all over the one pair of pants I always wear.

But still. It was like—I am putting you on notice. We were now the Andy Griffith and Barney Fife of Chicago.

A while after we got there, I met a guy who asked me, "Do you believe in dinosaurs?"

And I could tell that for some reason he didn't think Southern people believed in dinosaurs. So naturally I said no, I didn't believe in dinosaurs, because it's a lot more fun to mess with people than to be honest. And he believed me, because it's a lot more fun to talk to someone who doesn't believe in dinosaurs than someone who does.

This dude was a great comedian, which made me feel even better about trying to become one myself. I mean, he thought I was saying something totally crazy, but he didn't get offended at all. He just thought it was funny. Sure, he assumed I was a stereotype, but in a weird way he actually had a very open mind. He *liked* people who were different. He could be friends with anyone. That sounded like my kind of career.

And for the record, I do believe in dinosaurs. Until I don't.

After me and Michael Clay got our apartment set up, I got my start by taking stand-up classes at a place called the Comedy College, taught by the comic Jim Rauth. But in the meantime I also needed to make money. My mom and dad helped me out with a little spending money, but that luxury basement pad wasn't gonna pay for itself. And Michael Clay needed a paycheck so he could set aside cash for a church that didn't exist.

We didn't even have a car, so we got around using an abandoned shopping cart we found under a bridge. We rolled home groceries from a supermarket a mile away. Gourmet stuff like ramen and tuna and cheap hamburger we cooked on an old George Foreman Grill that a buddy had given us. When we got home, we'd lock up the cart with a padlock, because this was obviously the kind of neighborhood where folks bumped into cars, didn't leave notes, and drove off to probably make sacrifices to the devil.

So me and Michael Clay found jobs at this sports bar that was about to open called Jake Melnick's Corner Tap, right in the middle of everything, in the Magnificent Mile. A couple weeks before opening day, we went in and interviewed with the manager, a tall guy with a goatee named Willie. We sat down and he gave us this skeptical look.

"Do you guys have any experience working in large, fast-paced, high-end restaurants?"

Michael Clay was like, "Absolutely none." I said, "Well, I worked at an Applebee's for a while. So also, absolutely none."

But Willie ended up being a huge fan of country music, so for once it actually helped that everything Michael Clay said sounded like "Dueling Banjos" if no one was the winner.

We were Jake Melnick's very first employees. We helped it open its doors for the very first time. So we literally did it all—cleaned bathrooms, scrubbed down the ovens and the grills, even put the very first tables together, screws, screwdrivers, the whole deal. It was probably the closest thing I'd done to skilled labor in my life. Honestly, it's a miracle this place exists at all.

We didn't know too many people in town, so it became our second home. It was a real-life Cheers, where people could go when they got off work or maybe for a drink after dinner. This was back when you could still smoke inside businesses, and once it opened you could smell the smoke rolling out of the game room where everyone would play darts or pool or cheer on the Cubs on TV. The owner had a driver, a dude who was kind of a friend of the family, and the bar was named after him, I guess because they just liked the sound of his name. The real Jake Melnick was a short guy in glasses who would stop by sometimes and have a beer. A painted portrait of him hung on the wall. It was an awesome place with lots of regulars, everyone from bankers to construction guys, and it's still there today despite, you know, us. Of course, every time I go back, it's kind of like when you go back to your old high school. I get all excited, and no one there cares.

But just when we started to get into a groove in our new city, we ran into someone who was not charmed at all by our Southern ways. And that someone was gigantic rats that wanted to eat us alive.

Yeah, remember that scratching we heard behind our walls in the dump we loved? It went on for weeks. Then one night, me and Michael Clay got home and there was a giant hole in the middle of his bedroom wall, right above his dresser. We had no idea what to make of this thing. Down South, we had these tiny little mice that made cute little holes in your wall. You'd see one and go, "Hey there, little fella, you looking for a snack? Make yourself at home. You're adorable."

But this hole was massive. I mean *huge*. And it had all these jagged, sharp edges, like something with giant fangs was chomping its way through.

Michael Clay's eyes opened wide. "What the heck did that? A raccoon? Possum?"

I said, "Whatever it is, it wants to hang out. And maybe murder us."

We called up the landlady who wouldn't give us an air conditioner, and she calmly informed us that it was probably rats, and she'd be over in a few days to take a look.

A few days?

Me and Michael Clay looked at each other. At least during the day we'd have a shot against this thing. Not that we could beat it in a fight, but, you know, maybe we could outrun it or something. But at night? While we were asleep in our beds? If I felt something big and furry crawling up my leg, I would scream. Throw up. Pass out. Probably all three. Then I'd really be at its mercy. We had to do *something*. So we covered up the hole with his baseball glove. Then we pushed his TV against that. This seemed like an excellent plan for stopping giant homicidal rodents.

Well, later that night, while Michael Clay was sound asleep in his bed, that rat chewed right through his glove. And it pushed the TV out of the way. This was not a light TV. This was an old-fashioned tube TV. This thing basically had transistors that weighed about a ton each. And that rat treated it like an iPad. We didn't know what the rat did after it got out of the wall, and we didn't want to know. Probably bench-pressed our sofa a few times.

Over the next couple nights, the rat went ahead and made himself right at home. Between our kitchen and living room, there was this little utility room where the water heater was located, and that became his headquarters. Sometimes in the middle of the night you could hear him push open the closet's wooden folding door. He'd make this spooky, terrifying scraping sound as his little claws moved across the floor and made his way under your bed. I'd wake up, pull my covers around me tight, and stare wide-eyed at the ceiling until I heard him slowly scamper away. This was only a slightly better approach than the baseball glove.

In what was possibly the best timing ever, this was all going on right before my girlfriend Laura's first visit. Currently Laura is my wife, and I now know her well enough to know she is *less* squeamish than me. But these were early days, and she hadn't yet taken on the role of the man in our relationship. So me and Michael Clay decided not to say a word about the rat.

Which seemed like an excellent strategy until she was getting ready in the bathroom one evening, and I saw the rat scamper right across the floor.

Up until now this dude had only haunted my dreams. I hadn't seen him in real life. Well, seeing him was worse. This sucker was big and brown and I swear its eyes glowed red as blood. I must've gasped or

Me and Laura. Earlier that morning we were almost eaten by rats.

grunted or done something manly like that, because Laura called from the bathroom, "Nate? What's wrong?"

I squeaked, "Nothing!"

The rat ran right into Michael Clay's room and I slammed his door shut. Like, "He can deal with this when he gets home. In the meantime, Mr. Rat, help yourself. Maybe you wanna polish off that TV." Laura never found out, and now we are married and she is officially in charge of any rodent infestations in our home.

A little while after Laura went back to Tennessee, our landlady finally came by. Like, "Awesome, just in the nick of time!" She took one look at the hole in Michael Clay's bedroom wall and she goes, "Yep. Rats."

She had some dudes set traps in the little utility room. These weren't old-fashioned mouse traps, they were these rectangles with sticky patches on them. We asked the exterminator guys how these things worked, and they said, "Well, the rats get stuck on 'em, then they can't go anywhere, so they kinda starve to death, and then you throw 'em out."

All right then. That's neat.

But guess what? We actually caught one. We opened the wooden door one day, and there it was. Dead. And we had no idea what to do. This dead city rat was massive, it was disgusting, it had killed one innocent baseball glove, moved one large TV, and terrorized our nights—and now it was stuck there on this weird sticky rectangle. How were we supposed to handle this monster?

So Michael Clay goes, "All right. You go get a trash bag, then I'll use this broom to kinda sweep it into the bag."

Of course, this arrangement didn't feel fair to me, because it really seemed like Michael Clay should do everything, but I'm a good guy so I went along with it. I got the bag, I held it down near the floor, and he pushed the giant rat inside. And it moved.

The rat was alive. Very, very unfortunately alive.

Michael Clay screamed, but I did not. Or maybe it was the other way around. And maybe, just maybe my scream was very loud and high-pitched in a very girl-like way. But I can't be sure, because I don't really remember.

But I do remember us running out of the utility closet, knocking into the door, then slamming it shut behind us. It was absolute madness. We're hyperventilating, our hands are shaking, sweat is pouring off our faces, and we call up the landlady, and we yell, "WE GOT HIM! We got one rat!"

She goes, "Oh. Great. There's probably ten more where that came from."

Me and Michael Clay spent so much time at that sports bar, Jake Melnick's. So much.

I mean, yeah, it was our job. But it was kind of the center of our social lives too. Most of the people we knew in Chicago were from either Jake's or the classes we were taking. I started inviting work buddies to come watch my first shows at the Comedy College, where I was finally starting to get comfortable onstage.

We'd even hang out at the bar when we weren't on the clock. And why not? All our friends were there, they had bigger TVs and free snacks, and we hadn't found a single killer rat hiding behind the walls. Our manager Willie would say, "You guys have been working way too many hours. I should probably give you a raise." And we'd go, "Please let us stay here forever. You don't even have to pay us. Heck, we'll pay *you*. But just pocket change, because we're poor."

He even named the two of us Employees of the Month, and I can guarantee you it wasn't because we were good workers. We *definitely* weren't any good at security.

Late one night after me and Michael Clay closed up, we were coming out the back door into an alley when we heard a woman scream. I turned, and just a few feet away this dude grabbed this lady's purse and took off down the street. So I shouted at Michael Clay, "You see that!? That dude just grabbed that lady's purse and took off down the street!"

Because I have a real way with words.

But, I mean, this wasn't no love tap for a parked car. This was the big time, and it was happening on our turf. I felt this shot of adrenaline, my instincts took over, my brain shut down. Which is saying a lot. The lady said, "He's wearing a blue shirt and a brown hat!" So me and Michael Clay shrugged and took off after him. If we were gonna be the Andy Griffith and Barney Fife of this town, we were gonna do it right. Or basically exactly how they would do it.

We were peeking behind every trash can, looking into every doorway, shouting at every random person we passed. "Hey, did you see a guy in a blue shirt and a brown hat?"

"A lady got her purse stolen!"

"Blue shirt! Brown hat! BLUE SHIRT! BROWN HAT!"

Did anyone hear us? Did anyone answer? Did we even care? Honestly, I have no idea, but it was a heck of a lot of fun.

Here we were on the mean streets of Chicago. I mean, we didn't know this lady who got robbed. This could've been a setup, someone wanting to mug us for all our tips, we didn't have a clue. But we didn't care—back home, you help people, you trust people, so that's what we did.

Then we saw the guy. Right there, just walking down the sidewalk. Blue shirt and a brown hat.

Suddenly me and Michael Clay realized we were totally in over our heads. I mean, finding the dude was one thing—but we had no idea what to do next. Then a modern-day miracle occurred. Right down the street, idling at the corner, we saw a parked patrol car. As the thief kept walking ahead of us, we ran over to the car, knocked on the window, and started babbling away: "Blue shirt, brown hat! Blue shirt, brown hat! He stole a purse!"

But for some reason this cop decides to listen to us. Like, "Well, these boys do sound like extras from *The Dukes of Hazzard*—but something tells me I should take them seriously."

So while we stood there, he cruised down the street, pulled up next to the purse-snatcher dude, got out, arrested him, and put him right in the back seat. Me and Michael Clay were just staring, mouths open. Like, "How is this even happening right now?"

After the cop slammed the door shut on the thief, he motioned us over. He told me to walk with him to help look for the purse—and he told Michael Clay to keep an eye on his patrol car. No joke, this police officer goes, "Oh, and if the thief starts kicking out the window, you holler and I'll come back."

All right then. That's neat.

So I said, "Michael Clay, whatever you do, don't let him see your face! This dude could be dangerous! He'll find us!"

Michael Clay got super nervous. He turned away from the car, hiding his face in the shadows, like, "Please don't let this guy identify me." Meanwhile the cop and I couldn't find a thing. So we got back to his patrol car, and the lady was there now too, and here I am, Nate Bargatze, the new sheriff in town, going, "Sorry, ma'am, we did the best we could. We could not, however, recover the property in question." I really had the situation under control.

The cop shook his head, as if he's some grizzled old vet who's seen this sad story way too many times, and he went, "Well, because we couldn't find the purse, I'm gonna have to let him go."

To this day, I have no idea why the policeman needed the purse to press charges. I mean, we'd all seen this man do it. He had a blue shirt and a brown hat! How much proof do you need?

Me and Michael Clay are taking this in, we turn around—and there's the thief, sitting in the back of the cruiser, staring us dead in the eyes.

The two of us gulped. You could actually hear the gulp. And we said, "Officer, can you at least give us a two-minute head start on this dude?"

Yeah. The cop shrugged and gave us a head start of *maybe* three seconds. Me and Michael Clay pushed our way right by the lady—"Sorry it didn't work out! Good luck with all that!"—and bolted out of there. We then spent the next two years in Chicago, hanging out at Jake Melnick's, patching various holes in our apartment walls—and always looking over our shoulder for the thief with the blue shirt and the brown hat.

Eventually Michael Clay moved back to Tennessee. That girl I mentioned—the tall punk gal who thought he talked like a banjo—she went with him. He always likes to say that I got a comedy career there, and he got a wife. I'm pretty sure his accent still drives her nuts.

As for me, I stuck with the comedy class and took three eight-week courses. I became obsessed with stand-up. Then I saw the movie *Comedian* with my hero Jerry Seinfeld, where he called New York the stand-up capital of America. That settled it. I knew where my next stop was.

Good thing there's no rats or crime in that place.

NO MORE GUILT-TIPPING

Tipping situations will be the death of me.

My parents were raised Catholic, so I inherited Catholic guilt, even though I was raised Baptist. Basically I have the guilt of the Catholics and the strictness of the Baptists. The line that I allow myself to walk is a very tiny line.

When I was twelve, my aunt got married at a Catholic church. During communion, I went up there to get the bread, and I had no idea what I was getting into. Baptist church is easy—they just hand that bread right over to you, and you go about your day. Not here. The priest held up the bread for me, but when I went to take it, he wouldn't hand it over. He just stared at me. He had a death grip on this bread of life.

I started to panic, like maybe this guy *knows* I'm not Catholic. He can just sense it, and he's thinking, "This boy shouldn't be here! Stealing our bread!" Then after a few seconds of total awkwardness, I realized he was waiting for me to say something.

Well, I had no idea what to do. I went with being polite at first. "Please." "Thank you." "Have a good day." Nope. Just more blank stares.

I'm thinking, "Maybe a word from the Bible." So I said, "Jesus." Then, "God." Then the actual word "Bible." Nope. Nothing. But now I was getting better energy from the priest. He was giving me looks like, "You're going in the right direction, man."

It finally clicked. I said, "Um. Amen?" And he gave me the bread. Did I eat it? I honestly can't even remember, I was so embarrassed. I turned around and the whole church was staring at me. I mean, this process takes at most one second. I was there a full minute at least. I could feel their eyeballs piercing my soul with their judgment. Or who knows, maybe they just wanted me to move so the next guy who actually knew what to say could get his bread.

Either way, Catholics are great with guilt, and I got all of it.

Okay. Back to tipping. Sorry, did it take too long to get here? Tipping is actually the main point of this chapter, but that other information seemed very important at the time.

For the record, I am not against tipping. I waited tables, I delivered pizza, I moved people's stuff. I come from a world of tipping. And it's not about the money. I know everyone says that, but it's true. For me the problem is the entire process and the guilt that goes with it.

When I go into a place where there's even the slightest vagueness about whether or not I should tip, I get stressed. There's a soft-serve ice cream place we—meaning I—go to. (It might be frozen yogurt or it might be custard, but to me anything that's cold and comes out of a machine is ice cream, so that's what I call it.) This place is self-serve. So I'm the one who puts the ice cream in the cup. I put all the toppings on. I grab the spoon. I put it on a scale. They weigh it. The employee then turns an iPad around and shows me the price. I put my card in, and then it asks me how much to tip.

And now the agony begins. I *know* the employees didn't do much except weigh the results of my labor. *They* know they didn't do much. And I honestly don't blame them at all. I don't even blame the owner.

Maybe he just doesn't know the software or something. Maybe they don't even *know* they're asking for a tip. Because in no world based on logic and reason should I even be *thinking* about tipping these dudes. It makes no sense.

But here we are. I have been asked. The guilt has started. I would actually rather give this person $100 outside the store than deal with this current torture over three bucks. And so naturally I tip. I have to. I don't really even have a choice. Because if I do not tip, I will leave this store and spend the rest of my day thinking that *they're* thinking about me not tipping.

I know. There's a busy life going on in my head. It's exhausting.

This is why I was very excited many years ago when Laura and I decided to do our honeymoon at a resort in Mexico that was all-inclusive, which meant that everything was included in the single price you paid at the beginning of the vacation.

Everything—including tips. Which meant that no one would expect a tip, no one would ever ask for a tip, and I would never have to even *think* about tipping. That, as far as I was concerned, was the real vacation.

A vacation from my brain.

As soon as we got to the resort in Mexico, I could sense the anxiety melt away.

It felt like everything was free, even though we already paid for it. And by "paid for it," I mean we got half the money from friends and family who donated to our honeymoon fund, and then my wife paid for the rest. Because her money was now a part of my no-money. Heck, I was so relaxed I didn't even walk around with my wallet full of my no-cash.

But then on our first day, the bellboy brought our bags to our room. I was thinking, "Awesome, he'll drop them on the ground then be on his way." But once he put our bags down, he just stood there. And looked at me. And looked. And looked. Deep into my eyes, down to my very soul.

I was like, "What is happening here? He can't be waiting for a tip. He *can't*! Should I say something?" Like, "This is, uh, all-inclusive, right?" But that felt a little blunt. Maybe I should try "Amen." That worked on the Catholics.

Finally I just turned around and walked away, making absolutely sure not to peek back over my shoulder. I could feel his disappointment burning through the back of my shirt.

Then at the pool, waiters would come by to take our orders and bring out our food and drinks. They were so busy they never really stopped to wait, but it was too late. I was already messed up. I couldn't relax. When I was in the pool, a guy brought me a drink and he actually did pause—just to make sure I wasn't going to tip, I guess—but there was nothing I could do. I was in the water! No one has money on them in the water. Especially if they're me and they only have their wife's money anyway.

Later when we finished dinner, they didn't even bring us a check. We'd already paid, of course, so we were just supposed to walk away. But there was no finality to the meal. No closure. I couldn't feel good about it. In my head, I was picturing the staff walking back to our table hoping to find cash stuffed under a plate, then walking away devastated.

Next day, back at the pool. They kept offering me towels, and I *knew* they were doing it to make me feel guilty. I mean, I love having a lot of towels, but this was getting out of control. I would say thank you, and I finally decided to start subtly dropping how lovely it was to be staying at this *all-inclusive* resort. Then I'd make jokes about how *relieved* I was to not carry cash. But then I realized they didn't speak English—something I barely do also—so none of it worked.

And then it happened. I saw another guy tip. He held out cash, and they took it.

All I could think was, "Dude, what are you doing? There is a *system!*"

But it was over for me. I started tipping my wife's money left and right to anyone even close to me. Waiters, bellboys, cooks. I was handing out fives and twenties to people who didn't even work there. Like other people who were on vacation. Just cramming these sweaty bills into their hands, then they'd look at each other like, "This sucker thinks he has to tip! Doesn't he know it's all-inclusive?"

Honestly, though, I felt relieved. At least now I knew. I had some certainty. I could finally calm down because I'd wrapped my head around the fact that I'd be tipping for the rest of the trip.

That's all I really want. Some reassurance. If you're an all-inclusive resort and tipping isn't allowed, I want to know about it. I want Post-it notes stuck up everywhere that say "NO TIPPING ALLOWED!" I want a giant billboard that says if you get caught tipping someone, both the guest *and* the employee are immediately kicked out.

Or if I'm supposed to give your workers a thousand dollars for ice cream I served myself or for bringing me an all-inclusive towel by the pool—that's fine. Just tell me up front. Tell me exactly what I have to do. That's really all it comes down to. I just don't want to make another decision.

Told you it wasn't about the money. Especially when it's all Laura's.

RANDOM FOOD THING 3: YOU CHANGED, MCDONALD'S. YOU CHANGED.

McDonald's and I have had a long and happy relationship. For a while, I thought it was the perfect relationship. Then it all came crashing down like a burger packed with beef and lies.

Does that make no sense? Good. Now you know how I felt the day I was betrayed.

When I was born back in the 1900s, McDonald's wasn't just a place to go when you were in a hurry or there was nothing better—it was an actual restaurant. A special destination, a treat that real people went to just because they liked going there. Getting your first Big Mac was a rite of passage. Like, "I am finally big enough to eat this sandwich with two whole patties. I do not know what is in this special sauce, but I do know that eating it makes me a man."

I still remember when my parents said I was old enough to have my first Big Mac. It was a bigger deal than getting my driver's license, and probably happened around the same age.

McDonald's was always there for me, because McDonald's never changes. There is no celebrity chef. Heck, there isn't even a chef. A different person makes your meal every time, and every time it is the exact same meal. It is a factory assembly line of goodness. Also, when it comes to nutrition, there is that. It is there, I have been told.

Everyone has their go-to Extra Value Meal. The meal they depend on. The meal that defines who they are. I have two, because I am a complex person. For me, it's the Number One, the Big Mac Meal, for obvious sentimental reasons. And the Number Two, the Two Cheeseburger Meal. Because there are two of them. Not really sure if there's much more to say. Two is better than one, especially when it comes to cheeseburgers. It's pretty simple.

But that's kind of the point. You go to McDonald's because you have a problem, and that is you are hungry. So you walk under those Golden Arches and you pick the One or the Two. The Big Mac or the Two Cheeseburgers. You want adventure? You want to live on the edge? Try the Filet-O-Fish, which is really not as bad as you think it is. The only thing you really have to do is say "no onions," and for more insight into why that's important, please go to "Random Food Thing 2: I Hate Onions."

McDonald's is simple, it's easy, it's always the same, and it's perfect. Or at least it was, until a few years ago when they decided to blow it all up. Honestly, to this day I have not really recovered. I do not see a psychiatrist, but I'm pretty sure if I did they would tell me this is when my trust issues started.

I was somewhere in the US, I never can remember, and I went to the drive-thru to grab lunch, just like any other day. Heck, probably just like the five or six days prior. Yes. In a row. So I ordered my usual. I didn't even look at the menu. What's the point? I know what the menu is. I feel it. It is a part of me. It is stamped on my soul. All I had to do was open my mouth and speak.

"Yeah, I'll have a Number Two, please."

Which obviously is the Two Cheeseburger Meal. The fried bedrock of my diet.

I got my food and got back on the road. That's another plus about McDonald's, by the way—easy to eat while you're driving. So I opened up my bag, reached in for one of my two cheeseburgers, and what did I find but a Quarter Pounder with Cheese.

That's right. A Quarter Pounder with Cheese. This might sound strange, but in an entire lifetime of eating at McDonald's, I had never ordered a QPC. I'm being completely serious right now. I mean, I'd probably eaten a couple here and there. You know how it is—you walk by a McDonald's, minding your own business, and someone puts a QPC in your hand. So you eat it. It happens. That's life. And it's a decent burger, I guess. But come on now. I'm a Big Mac Guy. I'm a Two Cheeseburgers Guy. I am most definitely not a QPC Guy. That's just how it is.

I ate it, but I thought about it for the rest of the drive. I kept thinking it must've been my mistake. Somehow, some way, I must've messed up this order I'd made a million times before. That was the only explanation. Then I thought, "You know what, I'll just take a look the next time I go to McDonald's, whenever that is."

So the next morning, I pulled up to the drive-thru, and there it was. Right there on the big glowing board in bright white letters. The QPC Meal was now the Number Two. And the Two Cheeseburger Meal was the Number Seven.

They had just, like, changed it.

I was so upset that I talked into the crackly drive-thru microphone and asked the lady, "What's going on? When did y'all change it?" Like she was in the McDonald's family.

And the voice said back, "Sir, I'm sixteen."

It made no sense! The Two Cheeseburger Meal should *be* the Number Two. It's only logical! Two equals two! Even I know that! I think! By making two cheeseburgers equal seven, McDonald's wasn't just offending me, but math itself. And you do not want to make math angry.

Not only that, one of my favorite meals wasn't even in the top five anymore. I mean, you're honestly trying to tell me the McChicken should come before my Two Cheeseburgers? *The McChicken?* What kind of psychos are rolling up to McDonald's and going, "You know what? Let's not even consider a meal that offers not just one but two perfectly great burgers in a single order. Right now I've got a taste for *chicken*." These are probably the same people who pick grilled over fried. Simply un-American.

To this day, I do not know why McDonald's made this awful change. I can only assume it was done specifically to mess with me. If so, mission accomplished. Now whenever I order the Two Cheeseburger Meal, I actually have to think about it for two seconds. And let me tell you, it is brutal. Though the two cheeseburgers are still delicious.

THE DOG CHAPTER

Back when I was growing up in Tennessee in the eighties and nineties, owning a dog was very easy.

No one took their dogs on walks. That was ridiculous. Dogs walked perfectly fine all by themselves. No one cleaned up after their dogs. That's what God made grass for. It's nature's perfect dog toilet. People just let their dogs out, the dogs did their business, and at some point they came home. Dogs were just around. Being dogs. Doing dog stuff. On their own terms.

Don't get me wrong—everyone still loved their dogs. How can you not? Your dog is *obsessed* with you. Every time you walk in the door, your dog goes nuts, no matter how much of an idiot you are. He doesn't care if you've been gone five minutes or five days, he acts like you just got home from a war. Like, "You made us all so proud, the way you trudged through that minefield, threw yourself on a bomb, and saved the lives of your entire unit," and you go, "Dude, I just ducked out to buy a box of Sour Patch Kids for breakfast. Relax." Even then he's like, "That's okay, man. I personally think a diet based entirely on corn syrup is a very healthy life decision." And you say, "Gosh, I love you."

So we all loved our dogs. It's just that back then you could have that love without putting any work or thought into it. It was dumb, lazy, not-responsible love, and we liked it that way.

In fact, our first family dog wasn't even ours. He just kind of hung out in our neighborhood, picking through garbage, eating scraps, and my parents said, "How sweet, a stray homeless dog that lives in the trash. We should let him sleep with our children in their bed."

There is actually an old photo which may or may not be in this book depending on if my mom can find it, and it is of me, my brother Derek, and this random dog all snuggled up in our bed. Me and Derek are sound asleep, and the dog has this wide-eyed look on his face like, "Well, this happened." We didn't know if he had fleas, we didn't know if he had rabies, we didn't know if he had a name. The most we did was call him "Black Dog," because he happened to be a black dog. Now that I think about it, maybe that's why I called my old blue car "Old Blue." Because I'm so great with names.

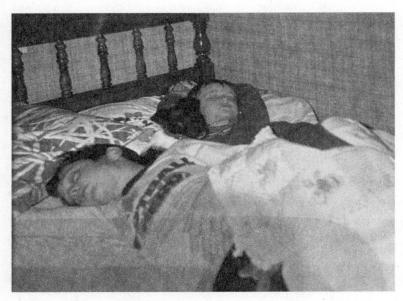

We found a picture of the picture. Good enough.

Black Dog slept in our house for a while, and then he went away, probably because he thought the trash outside smelled better than two little kids. But hey, at least I never had to take him for a walk.

If I'm being honest, even when we actually owned our pets I wasn't much better. When I was about nine years old I begged my parents for a snake. Begged. Had to have it. So on Christmas Eve my dad went to a guy's house and bought me a red tail boa. Apparently this dude just owned a bunch of snakes and had them in his house. How did my dad even find a guy like that? I mean, this was before the internet!*

Anyway, my dad's expecting this thing in a bag or a hazmat case or something, but the guy just hands him this boa constrictor and goes, "It's cold outside, so put him down your shirt and keep him close to your belly on the ride home." Like, "Skin-to-skin contact is very important for you to bond with this deadly reptile."

My dad's thinking, "Well, a man's gotta do what a man's gotta do." So he holds this snake against his bare chest, he gets home, and he goes, "Here you go, feed your snake," and I laugh and say, "You must be crazy." I mean, have y'all seen a red tail boa eat a live mouse? It's disgusting.

Most of the time we kept the snake—which we named "Snake"—in an aquarium in our house, but sometimes he needed exercise, so we'd let him out in our yard, just like a dog. My dad would play tricks on the mailman where he'd say, "Hey, is that a snake?" and then the mailman would run away screaming. When the mailman complained, my dad said, "Relax, it's just a little garter snake."

But it was not just a garter snake, so when Snake got big enough to eat a guinea pig or a rabbit or our little miniature schnauzer Noah we took Snake back to the owner. Thankfully Noah was not harmed, because this is not that kind of book.

---

*I still don't know how he did it, so I'm sorry to bring you all the way down here. You know, how about you just ask him when you see him.

We'd just bought Noah, who was the runt of a litter of miniature schnauzers, and we'd named him after Noah from the Bible to honor the man who'd saved the earth and its animals from an apocalyptic flood. Also because it was a step up from "Tiny Dog."

Me and Noah were close, but he was my sister Abigail's best friend. I knew they were best friends because he would even tolerate her obsession with the Spice Girls. I would actually overhear this ten-year-old girl having conversations with our dog like:

"Noah, can you believe Ginger Spice left the group?!"

Pause.

"You're right—you've always been a Baby Spice kind of dog."

But would my family walk Noah? Would we clean up after him? Heck no! No one did. It was unheard of back then. We're supposed to carry a little plastic baggie around? To do *what*?? Our whole town was one big minefield of dog poop, and everyone was fine with that.

It was the twentieth century, the grass was well fertilized, and as far as I was concerned, dumb, lazy dog love was the best kind of love in the world.

Then the twenty-first century rolled around, I moved to New York, and suddenly life and dogs got a lot more complicated.

I was twenty-five, and I'd spent the last year in Chicago living in a basement apartment, learning how to tell jokes in front of strangers, and having pro-wrestling fights with my buddies on our couch. I figured I was ready to be a man.

So I went to NYC and I asked my parents for money, because that's what real men do. I worked a little as a delivery guy during the day, and at night I tried to get onstage at the comedy clubs. Most important, me and my roommate Sven had a big yellow dog named Sasha. She was a mutt, and I am going to say she was one part Labrador and five parts shame. Ours.

In my defense, Sasha was technically Sven's dog. He brought her with him when he moved to the city. I did not go out and actively seek this additional responsibility.

In Sven's defense, I was all for it, because I was stupid. I had never taken care of a dog or even a snake without my parents' help before, but I said, "No big deal! Sure, we're two young dudes who are almost never home, who can barely walk and feed ourselves, and who are basically broke. But let's own a large baby who happens to have fur and a wet nose. We can do this!"

Then I realized that the New York of my adulthood was a lot different from the Tennessee of my childhood. First off, I started to notice that people all over the city seemed to, like, walk their dogs. With a leash and collar and careful adult supervision and also I guess common sense. Apparently, one was not supposed to allow one's dog to walk the streets, pooping at his leisure.

This was news to me.

Second, there was not much grass in New York. Dogs pooped on concrete sidewalks, which seemed barbaric to me. Not only that, but people stopped and *cleaned up* after their dogs. Every single time the dog did its business! That was just crazy.

They even had these special devices to do it—mechanical scoops and little rolled-up baggies that had been designed especially to pick up dog poop. Designed! With plans and patents! Someone went to engineering school and got a degree so they could create this stuff. For the first time ever I was proud I flunked out of college.

I tried my best to stop New Yorkers so I could ask them about all this new strangeness with dogs. But there was another thing about New Yorkers—they don't like to talk so much. Back in Tennessee, we'd take about ten minutes just to say goodbye to somebody.

"Well, all right then, I'll be seeing ya . . . "

"Yep, I'll be talking to ya . . . "

"All right, but make sure you say hi to Barb for me . . . "

"I will, I will. And I think we'll be seeing y'all at the fish fry . . . "

"Oh, that's right! The fish fry. When is that again?"

"I think it's after church next Sunday . . . "

"I like church . . . "

"Yeah. Me too. All right then . . . "

"What do you think of the new pastor?"

"Well . . . "

But in New York, I'd barely ask them what church they went to before they'd tell me to get to the point: "I'm in a hurry! Don't you see how much dog stuff I still got to clean up?" Then they'd find an open car window and honk the horn just for the heck of it. And I'd go, "I'm sorry, but in my town of Old Hickory honking is considered rude and it takes us at least twenty minutes to figure out right of way."

Me and Sven did our best to take care of Sasha the modern New York way. We really did. But we were both just getting started as comedians, and a comic's lifestyle is crazy.

I'd be out all day and all night, taking the subway from one place to another, popping in and out of clubs trying to get gigs. I'd be talking to my friends and I'd casually mention that I needed to get home to take out my dog, and their faces would go white with horror. "But—but we've been hanging out for the last thirty-six hours straight! Just take that poor animal for a walk! Seriously, you can leave. We don't even like you very much."

Finally I'd get around to going home, I'd walk through the door, and Sasha would jump up all happy and barking, like, "You made it! Back from 'Nam! I knew you'd pull through!"

My dumb, lazy heart would break from the guilt. Pretty much anyone else would offer her more stability than me. My dad was a professional magician. He literally made dogs disappear for a living. His idea of fun was terrifying our mailman with a boa constrictor. And even he understood that owning an animal is a real commitment that should not be scoffed at.

Me and Sven tried to make it work, but we just could not take care of Sasha. So I called up my parents and said, "Hey, do you want this dog?"

They said, "No."

I said, "Great, I'm buying Sasha a carrier and putting her on the next plane to Nashville."

Then I let them pay for it all. Really there's no comparison between a magician and a young, stupid comic when it comes to being responsible. The magician wins hands down, every time.

So really, he loses.

A couple years later, Laura moved to New York and we got married. So obviously it was time to try owning a dog again.

In my defense, I swear this was yet another dog I did not ask for. A comic I'm buddies with stopped by one day and said, "Hey, I found this dog wandering around. Want it?" Stuff like this happens to me so often that for a long time I assumed this was how it works for most people. Like, why do pet stores even exist? Doesn't every child just wake up with random black dogs in their beds? Doesn't everyone have friends who bring strange animals to their doorstep and go, "All yours! Might want to check for rabies!"

Laura of course knew all about how bad I failed with Sasha. She saw my old dog hanging out at my parents' house right before she made the move to New York, and Laura asked Sasha if she had any message for me. After everything I put her through, Sasha didn't even hold a grudge. Just panted, licked Laura's hand, and said, "Give that dude a Purple Heart for me." Which only made me feel more guilty.

Me and Laura had also been having our own issues with being responsible. And by "me and Laura" I mean "100 percent me." At this point, Laura was the only one of us making real money because she was the only one of us with a real job, working in, I don't know, business or something. The details were over my head. She was gone from morning till night, working, and she had this crazy idea that during this time

I should do, like, stuff. Take out the trash. Wash the dishes. All despite the fact that the dishwasher was broken, and I hate trash. Like I said, crazy.

Her solution was to leave me notes. So instead of her saying, "Nate, do the dishes and take out the trash," she would leave Post-its everywhere that said, "Nate, do the dishes and take out the trash." Her theory was "this way you will blame the note, and not me." I don't know if I agree with that. This note did not appear on its own. I know where this note is coming from. I also know that a small yellow piece of paper does not actually care if our dishes are dirty or clean. The Post-it is an innocent bystander in this argument. It is being framed.

My solution was to buy lots and lots of plastic plates and cups. Then I would throw them in the trash after I used them. Then I would not take out the trash.

Anyway, for some reason Laura was slightly skeptical that I would be able to take care of a dog. But as soon as I saw this dog, it was love at first sight. He was this little spunky brown-haired mutt and he had these big dumb eyes. So basically my son.

I told Laura we *had* to keep him. I promised I would feed him and walk him and clean up after him and everything. Laura said okay, but she would hold me to it. I named my dog Vandy, both because they're my favorite college football team, and because they also are a lost cause.

But guess what? I did the work, just like I said. I know. I am still shocked all these years later. But it's true. I did everything for Vandy, every day, right on time. And that dog was in love with me. Seriously. Every night, he would lie next to me in bed, and he would snuggle up against me as close as he could. He would put his head on top of my head, getting closer and closer until he was basically on top of my face.

Laura was tucked in there somewhere too, I guess. And that ended up being the problem. Because Laura *hated* Vandy, because she was jealous of our love. All right, mostly Vandy hated Laura, but it's more fun to blame my wife.

Vandy, though, wanted me all to himself. He gave Laura lots of atti-tude, he sulked, there was some passive-aggressive barking. Typical teen-ager stuff. I tried to talk to him about it. I said, "Son, I understand why you're jealous of your mom. But I promise that nothing will ever come between me and you. You're my kin. My blood. And nothing will ever change that."

Then this one time Vandy snapped at Laura, and even I understood that we needed to find him a better home. To be clear, this was *not a bite*. No teeth were involved. No skin was broken. Well, maybe there was a tiny scratch. You know how teens can be.

So Laura found him this nice lady who lived out on Long Island. Vandy would have a big yard to play in, and a nice, comfortable house. It would be a good life for my boy. The lady said she was gonna rename Vandy "Princess."

I was like, "Can you at least keep calling him Vandy? Please?"

Nope. Princess.

A couple years ago, the owner reached out to Laura on Facebook and said that Princess had just passed away after twelve long years of love, happiness, and health. I was sad. That could've been us. That could've been our love, happiness, and health. That could've been our dog, our son, and he could've been named Vandy instead of Princess.

Never could figure out why she'd name a boy dog Princess. Come to think of it, it's possible Vandy was a girl. Who knows. But we were close. So close.

Vandy left me a changed man. A little while later, I was getting into my car when I saw a dog running around down the street, no collar, no leash, no nothing. He looked happy enough, and he wasn't really both-ering no one. He was just out, roaming around, free in the wilds of New York to do his business wherever he wanted.

I looked around and saw a guy about thirty feet away who I didn't recognize. I didn't say hello. I didn't make chitchat. Didn't ask how his day was going or what church he went to or if he was new to the neighborhood. I just shouted, "HEY! Is that your dog?? He needs a leash!"

He looked at me confused. Like, "Who is this crazy dude who's yelling at me to take care of random stray dogs on the street? They can poop wherever they want, for all I care!" I sighed, shook my head, and got in the car. I finally understood what it took to own a dog, but some guys would just never get it. Not like me.

Still never took out the trash, though.

I really thought I had the whole "taking care of your dog" thing down. So when me and Laura moved back to Tennessee, we took a stab at owning a dog that liked both of us, and instead we ended up caught in a true-crime murder mystery.

Because that's what happens when you try to be a good pet owner. Your dog goes ahead and gets accused of murder. So I guess this *is* that kind of book.

We got this dog from my sister Abigail, who is the animal lover of the family. She was working as a vet's assistant, so she was always coming across rescues and trying to find them homes. Annie was an older dog, white coat, maybe ten. She was technically a bird dog, but her former owner said she was horrible. Like she'd always get in the way of the guns instead of going after the birds. So me and Laura said, "She'll fit in just fine here."

Not that Annie was stupid. But I will say before this jury of my peers that it is true that Annie was a little . . . well, something was off. I mean, not a *bad* off. She was sweet to the point of being simple. She never barked, she was super mellow, and she was named after Little Orphan Annie because she always looked lost and she seemed to enjoy musicals. Our daughter Harper, who was three at the time, would lie directly on top of her and cover her with stuffed animals, and Annie would never even blink. So, all right, maybe she was kinda stupid. Which, Your Honor, is exactly why she *cannot* be guilty of the crime she has been accused of.

Annie and Jude: a tangled web.

The details of the case are as follows.

It was an afternoon on a day like any other. We were out of town, so Annie was staying at Abigail's place. Abigail went out, and Annie was left alone with her dog Jude and my parents' cat Cosmo, who was also visiting.

Jude had an impeccable reputation as what is commonly called a "good dog." He was a TBM, which I thought was a fancy breeding term, but my sister now tells me means "Tennessee brown mutt." My sister named him after the Beatles song, and she would always sing, "Hey Jude, don't poop on the floor," because she thought it was funny and not because Jude ever pooped on the floor. We can at least be happy that she'd moved on from the Spice Girls. Cosmo was a cat named after the character in *Seinfeld*, so her full name was technically Cosmo Kramer, but no one ever called her that. She was a tabby, and she was fat. These are the facts of the case, and they are not in dispute.

When my sister got home that day, Cosmo had apparently been . . . well, this is family entertainment. I really do not want to say she was murdered. So let's just say that she was asleep, all right? And I mean asleep for a long time. Like asleep forever. And in a place called Kitty Heaven. But still—definitely only asleep.

Annie was apparently standing over the, uh, sleeping Cosmo with what my sister claimed was a "guilty look" on her face, and, um, Kool-Aid all over her white fur. Like red Kool-Aid. I mean *very* red Kool-Aid. I mean I think this flavor was Blood Red Kool-Aid. And there was a *lot* of it. Like she just guzzled a whole big glass pitcher of the Kool-Aid Man himself, and those red Kool-Aid guts got everywhere. Annie had no emotion. She was just kind of hanging out, watching Cosmo, you know, sleep. Forever.

Jude, on the other hand, was off somewhere, totally clean, not pooping on the floor, being, as always, a very good dog.

The DA on this case—let's call her Abigail, which also happens to be my sister's name—says the case is open and shut. Annie is guilty as charged. Plain and simple. I, however, say this is nothing but a doggy version of *Making a Murderer*. And if you haven't watched *Making a Murderer* in a while, I highly recommend that you watch it right now, because it's good and also so you get this reference.

Yeah, I get that it looks bad. Real bad. But do we honestly think that Annie is smart enough to pull something like this off? No way. I mean, this is a bird dog who chases the gun instead of the birds! This dog doesn't have a mean or intelligent bone in her body.

But that Jude . . . yeah, he seems like a good dog all right. Always says the right thing. Never poops on the floor. Puts up with my sister's singing. But he's capable of a lot more than he lets on, I guarantee it. There is a devious criminal mastermind hiding behind those big brown eyes and that wet tongue. Whatever happened that day—whoever *technically* made Cosmo, uh, go to sleep—I guarantee you Jude was the one pulling the strings.

Like he's saying, "Hey, my slow but well-meaning nephew—look at that Cosmo over there. Don't he look all nice and fat and tasty? Ain't he just asking for trouble?"

And Annie goes, "Gosh, Uncle Jude, I just want to go watch some WWE."

And Jude goes, "Sure, kid. Have some Kool-Aid."

Annie passed a few years back. She died of cancer, which was very sad, but at least it did not involve any fruit-punch-type drink of any kind. To the very end, she was pretty dumb and totally unable to catch any birds. And to my dying day, no matter what the evidence or the viewers of Netflix say, I will be convinced of her innocence.

For her part, Abigail insists that Cosmo the cat was old and grouchy and probably started the fight anyway, which I'm sure is something Jude whispered to her the night of the crime. She is, and always will be, the family animal lover, but this is her one blind spot.

Jude is, she claims, a really, truly good dog.

Once Harper got older, me and Laura got her her own dog to teach her responsibility too. That's going about as well as it did for me when I moved to New York.

Up until this point we'd always have rescues and mutts. But now all of a sudden we had to have a doodle named Holly. Everyone's got a doodle. The whole neighborhood is full of them. Labradoodles, golden doodles, everything doodles. It's how you know you're in the suburbs.

Not only does everyone own one, but everyone has the same excuse for owning one. Suddenly we all broke out in these extremely violent allergies to normal, ugly dogs. You ask someone about their doodle and it's always, "Well, we really wanted to get a rescue . . . but our whole family is allergic so we had to get a doodle."

I mean, twenty years ago none of these so-called allergy people were going out and buying up hairless cats and going, "What could we do? We sneezed a few times so we had to buy this plucked chicken with paws." But now that doodles are around it's like, "Well, we could go to the rescue and get this mutt with one eye and a bad leg who sheds hair like straw all over the house. Or we can get the Lamborghini of dogs."

These things don't shed, they come neutered and trained and capable of understanding commands in more languages than I can speak. So, one. I wanted to let Holly out back to do her business and Laura looked at me horrified. "Two weeks ago on Nextdoor, someone said they saw a fox! How do you possibly think a doodle is gonna survive a fox? It probably has atrocious table manners!" These dogs aren't animals. They aren't even dogs anymore. They're people. They're members of the family.

But does Harper do a single thing to take care of her puppy sister? Of course not. She's supposed to walk her and feed her every day, but she never does. Because I am now a responsible person, I am the one who walks her. And I believe someone does feed her. I really don't know who, or even where the dog food is located in our house. But Holly seems healthy enough, so I assume it happens.

I am fine with the dog walking, especially because I am trying to get in shape right now, because I am always trying to get in shape right now. In principle, I'm even fine with the poop-scooping. Sure, back in the eighties and nineties we were all okay walking around and stepping on poop in our yards. But we were simpler folk back then. Stronger. One with our land and our lawns. Times change. Attitudes evolve. Now we're too fancy to walk around with dog poop on our shoes. Some might call us spoiled. I could complain about our society's moral decay, but I will not. I will pick up after Holly like a good citizen.

That said.

Does this highly trained sports car of a dog really have to go so *much*? With all the breeding and the science stuff the scientists did to make the doodle the perfect dog, could they not have given it a stronger stomach? Is that too much to ask?

Here I am, trying to get some exercise in, trying to be healthy for once in my life, and Holly won't even let me run at a decent pace. Which I honestly don't mind, because what sane person actually likes to run—but still! As soon as my heart rate gets up, she has to go. It's just stop-start, stop-start for two solid miles. I can barely burn off half of the six Krispy Kremes I had for breakfast.

Laura says it's my fault. She says, "You just have to keep Holly on the sidewalk! Don't let her sniff the grass, because that's when she has to go!"

Seriously—have you *tried* to stop a dog from sniffing grass? You could be walking a tiny little chihuahua, and as soon as that thing gets a whiff of turf he turns into a pit bull on steroids. You are not moving him an inch. He will drag you to your death if there's something in the dirt he wants to smell, and you will not be able to stop him.

Laura's like, "Well, isn't tugging on Holly's leash just like working out with resistance bands? Think of it as exercise!"

Really? I'm exercising to look *better*. Do I really want my neighbors staring at me as I struggle with every muscle of my body to drag a medium-sized doodle down a sidewalk?

"All right," she says, "so each time you pick up after her, do a squat. There's your exercise."

At this point, I don't think my wife understands the urgency of this situation. This dog goes so much I actually run out of baggies when we're on a walk. I took three baggies last time. Three baggies! It still wasn't enough! I'd blame it on whatever we're feeding her, but I have no idea who to even talk to about that dog-feeding process.

Plus, I am only able to do two squats on any given day. Or week, actually.

When you run out of baggies, that's when you're really in trouble. Then you gotta do the whole "hidden shrub shuffle." Holly's about to do her business, I realize I've got no baggies left, and we're right in the middle of someone's yard, in full view of the entire neighborhood. I know this stuff ain't getting picked up, Holly knows this stuff ain't getting picked up, and all our neighbors are about to know it too.

So I'm trying to drag her, mid-squat, back behind some hidden shrub so no one can see the crime we're about to commit—and this is even harder than dragging her away from sniffing grass. I'm going, "Nothing to see here, folks! Move along! Just trying to get some exercise in! It's band work!"

Holly, of course, never makes it behind the hidden shrub. So there's her poop, right there in the middle of this dude's lawn, and I'm feeling so guilty that after we get home I get in my car and drive back all by myself just so I can pick up my daughter's dog's poop. Like, Netflix ain't gonna make a documentary about *me* getting framed for this dog's lawless ways.

I finally get back to the house, and there's Harper, lying on the couch watching TV, with Holly curled up right next to her, snuggled in tight. No one's excited to see me. No one's jumping up and down. There's no panting, no energy, no enthusiasm. They barely even look up from the TV. It's like I got two little humans, lying there being adolescent girls together.

"Harper," I say, "do you got any idea what I've just been through out there?"

"Daddy," she goes, "you took Holly for a walk around the block. What do you want—a medal?"

NO RUNNING IN THE MADHOUSE

About fifteen years ago, my parents paid for the whole family to go to Disney World.

No one knows exactly where they got the money from, and to this day if you ask my dad he says mysterious things like, "When you're a professional magician like me . . . you know people who know people."

Of course it was a special treat for the kids. This was before my daughter Harper was born, but my sister's boy Caleb and my brother's daughter Esther were two and three. And honestly all they wanted to do was see the princesses. All the other Disney characters were a no-go—Mickey, Minnie, Pluto—because Caleb was absolutely terrified of the costumes. Which I totally get. You try getting down close to the floor and staring up into a giant mouse's nostrils and see how much you like it.

But there was a problem. The line to see the princesses was three hours long to basically say "hey" to Cinderella. Also my dad's Magic Mafia apparently has no power over royalty. So we went to the back to wait like everyone else.

Thirty minutes go by, the line doesn't feel like it's getting any shorter, and even the toddlers are starting to question the meaning of life, when

Me and my brother with Tigger. See? Terrifying.

suddenly this random guy comes up to us and goes, "Hey, I've got two children's tickets for that much shorter line over there. My girl got sick and we can't do it, so y'all want our tickets?"

The rest of us kind of give each other this look like, "Is this dude for real?" This sounds way too good to be true, like maybe it's a scam or something. But my dad goes, "What's life without taking risks?" So without any questions, he turns to the guy, says, "Thank you very much, kind sir," grabs the tickets, and whisks us away. I'm just thinking, "I will never talk bad about this League of Magicians again."

We go back where this dude pointed, and it's true—there's almost no line there at all. We flash our tickets to the person at the door, they look at our two kids, and it's just, "Come right in! Come right in! Welcome! Make yourselves at home!"

So we shrug and say, "Cool. All right."

We walk into this place, and not only do Caleb and Esther get to say hi to Cinderella, this is the craziest, most complete Disney princess experience you've ever seen. I mean, you got every princess in history sprinting out to meet us. You got Snow White, you got Ariel, you got Belle, you got princesses no one's even heard of, like Sue or Nancy, they're just side characters from movies that went straight to video. And they just mob our kids with attention, they surround them like this pink, glittery storm of love.

They ain't just saying "hello" and moving on. These princesses are having full on heart-to-heart talks with Caleb and Esther: "What's your name? Where are you visiting from? Tell us your dreams, tell us your hopes. Our entire royal court is here for you. Whatever you want—name it, and it's yours!"

The kids are soaking all this up. To them, these are the *real* princesses. The actual ladies who somehow jumped out of the movies and are standing right in front of them in flesh and blood and very pink dresses. Just as important to Caleb, they are not gigantic mice or ducks or whatever Goofy is. So they're hugging these princesses, hanging on their every word, completely mesmerized. Like *more-more-more*! Please make this last *forever*!

The grown-ups are all loving this too, of course. Who wouldn't love to see their kids get treated so special? But after twenty minutes it starts getting a little weird.

My sister Abigail nudges me and says, "Hey, why do all the princesses have tears in their eyes? I just saw Pocahontas sobbing in the corner."

Then Sleeping Beauty walks up to my dad and whispers, "You're so strong. We just know you guys will make it."

My dad kinda hesitates and says, "Yeah, um. Having two grandkids is a lot of work."

Then I see him peek at this clipboard that Sleeping Beauty is holding. His eyes open wide, his jaw drops, and he goes, "I gotta get out of here!"

Without another word, he bolts. I mean he just sprints out that door, leaving us in the dust. The rest of us have no idea what's going on. Like—is this a bathroom emergency or something? We finally wander outside after the princesses praise our courage for bearing children a few more times, and my dad is standing there horrified.

"Make-A-Wish," he gasps. "That was the line for Make-A-Wish. That guy's kid wasn't sick—he was *sick*. They probably thought Caleb and Esther had cancer or something!"

We cannot believe what we're hearing. We obviously had no idea what the special tickets were for, but now we feel like the worst people on the planet, especially because we could've got out of there fifteen minutes earlier. We go, "Dad, why didn't you tell us?"

"Well," he says, thinking. "Your mom would've ratted us out."

To this day, I volunteer for Make-A-Wish whenever I can. I mean constantly. All the time. Seriously—Make-A-Wish people, if you are out there, I will do something for you *tonight*.

Just say the word.

Our family, like all healthy Americans, is very into going to theme parks and county fairs and other fun events. My dad, like other unhealthy fathers, is very into making us do a bunch of crazy stuff we don't want to do. Rides, games, roller coasters, accepting tickets for sick kids. Saying things like, "Y'all chicken? This is life! You gotta be tough!"

Then when it was his turn, he'd go, "What do you think I am, some kind of idiot?"

We thought he was a professional magician. But by the time we tried to answer he'd usually pushed us ahead of him in line.

My dad started in on me at an early age. Specifically, when I was still in the womb. My mom was about five months pregnant with me when Halloween rolled around. My dad said he wanted to take her to a haunted house in downtown Nashville. And this was when downtown

Nashville was a haunted house in of itself. My mom said, "You know those things scare me to death. Besides, what about the baby?"

My dad goes, "Never too young to toughen him up!"

So they went to this place, which was in this old brick building on Main Street across from a Krispy Kreme. They walk inside, and it's these tight, pitch-black hallways with all these "inmates" from an insane asylum screaming and reaching their hands out to grab you as you walk by. My dad takes one look at this madness, and he grabs my mom and pushes her in front, shouting, "Ladies and babies first!"

I probably would've been traumatized, but even then I could sense the hot sticky Krispy Kremes across the way. Terror never smelled so delicious.

When me and my siblings got older—like, past being born—my dad would make all of us do the haunted house with the usual crazy inmates and scary stuff at the county fair. He'd act like getting the bejesus scared out of us was somehow teaching us this powerful life lesson. One year he gathered us at the entrance and started preaching. "Never, ever run. Remember, kids—there's nothing to fear but fear itself."

Then when we got inside, he found the chainsaw guy and said, "Leave me alone, but you got my permission to go after these children."

That chainsaw guy came at us screaming and howling and waving the chainsaw in the air. Me and my sister only saw fear itself, so we stayed put. But my brother Derek and his buddy Brandon saw a man with a chainsaw, screaming and howling and running after them. They took off at a sprint and didn't stop until they reached the parking lot.

We found them twenty minutes later hiding in the back of a pickup truck owned by a strange man. My dad wanted to give the man permission to just drive away, but my mother said maybe it was time to go home.

She was like that, my mom. Always trying to protect us. I guess the motherly bond includes making sure your young don't get murdered by a madman with a power tool. She didn't stop with haunted houses, though. She was against any park ride that turned, twisted, shook, spun around, or moved more than a foot. So basically all of them.

"Well," she'd say, eyeing a carousel suspiciously, "I just read about five people dying on that thing in Japan. Apparently the horses went on a rampage."

"All right," she'd say when we got to the teacup ride. "But I'm pretty sure a cup like this broke apart in Slovakia just last week. Made of real china, I believe."

Or when we got to the fifty-year-old roller coaster at the county fair: "Couldn't we find something where there aren't workers hammering on it literally right now?"

Maybe mom had a point on that last one. That coaster was big and white and made of wood, and it was always broken. Which wouldn't have been a big deal, except the fair always kept it running anyway. You'd be climbing up the first steep hill, and you'd hear this *BAM! BAM! BAM!* coming from somewhere. You'd reach the peak and there would be a shout: "Think that cracked rusty gear will hold?" Then right when you hit the bottom you'd hear, "Guess so! This time!"

But for some reason none of this bothered me and my brother. Sure, the ride was fast and terrifying and possibly deadly, but that seemed like half the fun. We were young, we figured we'd live forever, and we'd already survived a serial killer with a chainsaw. What did we have to lose? And my dad, of course, was all for it. Not just because riding a death trap would obviously turn us into real men, but because it only cost a dollar per ride. In a weird coincidence that is definitely only a coincidence, my father's tough love is very cheap.

So me and Derek would be screaming on this thing as the workers tried to figure out what was wrong with the brakes, and my dad would shout, "I got a buck left if we need urgent care!" Followed by, "But if you can walk it off, even better!"

Sometimes he paid to get into the park using Coke cans, which was a promotion they liked to use. *Buy a Cherry Coke, get dismembered for free!* In that case, if we got injured the plan was to rub caffeine into our wounds.

Lucky for us, we always had fun and came away only a little emotionally scarred. Diet Dr Pepper is great on a sprain, but not so good for therapy.

My sister Abigail was a little smarter than me and Derek.

She thought back to when my dad taught her to swim by going to the YMCA, having her go off the slide into the deep end, and telling the lifeguard, "Just give her a second. She'll figure it out." If anything I'm surprised he didn't give the guy a chainsaw, just to keep things interesting.

Abigail did figure it out, thankfully, which I know because she is still alive today. She also figured that she would never, ever let my dad get her on a roller coaster. If he could take a little swimming pool slide and make it scary, what would he do with a ride that was actually *supposed* to be scary?

This drove my dad nuts. Again, because of the very moral principle that he is very cheap. Getting a pass to the Opryland Theme Park cost the same if you rode all the rides or if you rode none of them. So to him, riding all the rides was the only way to get your money's worth. If you didn't ride everything you could possibly ride, no matter what it was, the park owners were "getting one over on you." Even if we got in using a Coke can deal, it was, "This sip of soda should've been a trip on the Grizzly River Rampage! They're getting one over on us!"

At the time, though, my sister had an easy out. You had to be forty-eight inches tall to ride the scariest stuff. She was only forty-six inches tall. Two inches too short. Even my dad couldn't argue with a height restriction. But he finally figured out her weakness. Which is quite the statement when you realize that my sister was only eight years old. I don't know, maybe just give her some ice cream? How hard can it be? But this is what our father spent his time doing—coming up with elaborate schemes to get second graders to bend to his will.

Like most little girls, Abigail wanted more than anything to be a big girl. Wear heels. Put on some makeup. That kind of thing. But we were Christian in the South, so as far as my parents were concerned she'd be fine in a nice tasteful gingham until she was twenty-five. Until one day when my dad treated her to the biggest surprise of her young life: her very first pair of heels.

In a weird coincidence that was definitely only a coincidence, my dad gave her this special gift on the same day we were going to Opryland. My sister wasn't born yesterday. She'd grown up a lot over those first eight years of sinking or swimming. So she looked at those heels and said, "Two inches high. Seems a little suspicious."

But my dad told her not to worry, and he walked her right over to a line he said was for "the swings." It was actually for the Hangman. A roller coaster that hung you upside down and raced you down a 103-foot drop through a sidewinder twist at fifty miles an hour.

So basically the swings, but with the death penalty.

They got to the front of the line, and thanks to those stylish two-inch heels the dude running the ride decided my sister would probably not have her head chopped off if she got on the Hangman. Probably.

But I gotta give Abigail credit. As terrified as she was, she kept it together. She took a deep breath, they did the ride, my dad got his money's worth, and my sister ended up loving it. And also not dying. She still enjoys riding the scary rides to this day.

For his part, our father wants to be crystal clear that when he tricked his eight-year-old daughter into maybe endangering her life, he did not in fact give her heels but just "sneakers with very thick soles."

Glad we could set the record straight.

If I'm being honest, even if we stayed away from pop-up insane asylums and roller coasters that killed people in Japan, the county fair could still be pretty risky.

Not in a crime way. This was back in the day when you could take your little kids to a fair or festival or something, say, "All right then, guess I'll be seeing y'all," and you knew you'd find 'em again. Maybe a couple days later, but you'd find 'em. My buddy Ryan's dad would take us to Walmart sometimes, not even to shop, just for the afternoon. And he'd go, "Have fun, boys. Listen for the whistle."

Then we'd just wander around looking at toys and various produce until we heard his shrill whistle echoing throughout the store. Or sometimes over the loudspeaker, "Would the two boys here with this whistling man come to the front? He is driving us crazy. Please make him stop."

No, everything was pretty safe like that. But it was not as safe for donkeys. For two or three years in a row, my dad took us to see one of the county fair's main attractions—a donkey diving from a platform way high up into a big pool of water down below. I could be wrong, but I believe that the donkeys did not do this by choice. I do not think that the event organizers went around to all the farms and interviewed livestock to see who had lifelong dreams of performing at SeaWorld.

To be clear, the donkeys always seemed fine. They'd take a jump off that platform, land in the water, then pop right out. But some animal-rights activists protested, so the county fair people said they'd learned their lesson and would immediately switch to fighting orangutans.

This one actually was dangerous—not for the orangutans, but for the folks who signed up to fight them. That is correct. The fighting orangutans were not fighting each other, they were fighting people who came to the county fair. And those people got beat up. Every single time. It was a fair fight that was not a fair fight. And now you know why I do not do puns.

The most surprising thing about all this is that my dad never tried to convince any of his children to fight an orangutan. Though I do have a vague memory of him purchasing foot-high platform shoes so Abigail could make the height limit.

Eventually the protesters got that shut down too, but the county fair people totally learned their lesson this time and immediately switched to pig races.

The winning hog gets to ride the broken white roller coaster.

A couple years ago, after a lifetime of daring the rest of us to go on the scariest, most dangerous rides in the world, my dad finally met his match—a little English dude in Orlando, Florida, by the name of Harry Potter.

You always gotta watch out for the ones in glasses. Very tricky people.

The Harry Potter ride at Universal Studios is what they call a "motion simulator," which I cannot actually speak out loud, but which basically means "this is barely even a ride." You get in a car, you move around a tiny bit, you tilt, you shake, you stare at a 3D screen, and that's it. Or so they tell you.

I'd had one of my own run-ins with these innocent-seeming death traps a few years earlier while visiting the other Universal Studios in Los Angeles. My experience was with the Simpsons ride, which was supposed to take me, my wife Laura, and our daughter Harper through a simulated 3D tour of Springfield. But which instead took me directly into my darkest and wildest fears. So a real treat.

Me, Harper, and Laura got on the Simpsons ride, we pulled the safety bar over our laps extra tight—and suddenly I felt trapped. Pinned down with no way out of this really tight space, plus this complete loss of control. It felt like I had to get off this machine. Right now. So I waved my arms for help, thinking, "I guess I'm that guy now. The arm-waving guy who makes everyone wait while they stop the ride."

I figured at least I was in California, where people surf and eat sushi and are understanding. If this happened in the South, I'd never hear the end of it. My dad would go, "You didn't even use your ticket? Man, Universal really got one over on you."

Claustrophobia actually became a thing for me. To the point where I'd get on crowded planes and freak out because I couldn't get off. I'd have to trick my brain. I'd take my seat, I'd take a deep breath, and I'd think, "I will eventually get off this plane. Even if it falls into the ocean. Even if it crashes into a mountain. I will get off. Sure, I might have all my bones broken, and I might need to get all my skin replaced, and I might never watch *The Simpsons* again, but somehow, someway, I will get off."

Or I'd take a Xanax. That also worked pretty good.

My dad figured he'd have no problem with these silly rides that didn't even go anywhere, so when he was at Universal in Orlando he hopped right onto the Harry Potter ride with his cousin. They pulled the safety bar back over their laps—not too tight, just to be sure—and they sat back to enjoy their 3D tour of, like, magic or whatever.

Barely moving more than a few inches, the car seemed to fly through the air, twisting and turning its way into Hogwarts. My dad said, "Oh."

Still hardly even budging, that car seemed to zoom around a few towers, whip past a dragon or two, go up and go down. My dad said, "Uh-oh."

Then they went by the great hall or whatever and probably waved at Ron and the old wizard dude, and then my dad threw up.

My dad threw up, and he threw up some more. His hotel had a free buffet, and my dad had eaten enough for three meals that morning. So he kept throwing up.

People around him started screaming, "That man is throwing up on us!" so an attendant rushed over to help my dad off the ride, and my dad threw up on him too.

My dad was scheduled to perform a magic show just a couple hours later, and he didn't have time to go to the hotel to change out of his clothes. So he went into a public bathroom, took off his shirt, his pants, and his socks, and he washed them all by hand in the sink. He put his clothes back on, went outside, and lied down on a bench until the sun dried him off.

He never went on another ride of almost any kind ever again. Heck, he can barely even see a movie in a theater anymore. Just the thought of staring at a big screen in the dark is enough to make him queasy. When he got back to Tennessee and told us the story, my mom said, "Even I haven't heard of anyone dying on one of those things."

But to this day my dad still does everything he can to make sure his kids and his grandkids go on every single ride, walk through every haunted house—no running allowed—and accept every free ticket from random strangers. And he always reminds us that even on that last, extremely pukey Harry Potter ride, they didn't pull him off until the very end.

So he definitely got his money's worth.

THE BET

A few days before my daughter Harper was due to be born, my mom and my wife made a bet about me. One of them would win. I would lose no matter what.

It was July 2012, and even though me and Laura still lived in New York at the time, Laura had been staying at my parents' house in Tennessee because we wanted to be close to family. And because we wanted Harper to be born in the South, because I didn't want her to grow up thinking she was better than me. Of course, now that we actually live in Nashville, she loves going on to all her friends about how she "used to live in New York," even though that lasted about a month, but, you know, other than that my plan worked perfect.

Anyway, once Laura got set up at my folks' place, the two of us went and found her a good new Southern doctor to deliver the baby. This guy seemed smart and doctory, he talked with a nice little twang—it was all going great. Then he looked at me and goes, "So, after the delivery will Dad want to cut the baby's umbilical cord?"

My jaw dropped. And just like that, my mom and my wife had their bet. Laura bet that there was no way I was cutting that cord. My mom said that when the moment of truth arrived, I'd be able to do it. "A mother knows her son," she said. "Nathan will cut that cord."

"Right," Laura answered. "A million bucks then?"

Honestly, my mom was lucky Laura didn't go for a cool ten mil. I said, "Mom, I don't think you know me as well as you think."

She was gonna have to cash in her retirement plan to pay this one off.

I'm very squeamish when it comes to anything that's gross. And by "gross," I mean blood and guts and definitely birth. This is something my mom should've been aware of.

I know a lot of people have a hard time getting shots or being around open cuts. But I can't even think about it. I can't see scars, I can't see scabs. I can't even see pictures or TV shows with blood in them. I don't just mean weird surgery stuff on the Discovery Channel. I mean fake stuff like *ER*, which is my mom's favorite program of all time. She'd be in the middle of an episode, and I'd walk in and gag. "Mom, someone's head is wide open!"

"You know it's not a real head, right? That's a rubber brain covered in ketchup or something."

"You ain't making things better!"

My mom loves *ER* so much she told us she wanted Harper to call her "Gammy" because Dr. Carter calls his grandmother Gammy on the show. Now, we don't do sentimental nicknames in our family. We just don't. There's no Paw-Paw or Mee-Maw or Hoo-Haw or whatever. Not that there's anything wrong with being sentimental, that's just not our thing. It's always been Dad. Mom. Grandpa. Grandma. I'm talking for generations.

But because Noah Wyle called some random old lady who played his grandmother "Gammy" once on some random episode, now this is our tradition, and now whenever my daughter talks to her grandma I think about an open rubber brain with ketchup blood and gag. (My mom also wants me to make it clear that in other episodes, Dr. Carter has apparently called his grandmother "Gamma." So maybe she got it wrong.)

To be fair, it's not my fault I'm so soft. It's my mother's fault for letting me be so soft. Since I was her firstborn, her natural instinct was to use bubble wrap as my baby blanket. Lucky for me, I did not suffocate. A few months after I was born, the doctor told her I was pigeon-toed, or as she likes to put it, "Your right foot was turned in funny." I was just this tiny little thing, and the doctor said I'd need to wear a tiny little baby cast for a while, then after that a pair of special white Stride Rite baby shoes with a metal bar connecting them to straighten me out, because if you're born in 1979 a torture device is the best they got.

This really should not have been a big deal, but on hearing the news, my mother burst into tears and called my dad crying because her perfect baby boy was gonna have to wear a cast and a brace for the first year of his life. My dad started crying because Stride Rite shoes are so darn expensive. I started crying because everyone else was crying, and it's been downhill for me and medical stuff ever since.

After that not-traumatic trauma, my mom only babied me even more. I got whatever I wanted, no matter how crazy. Most famously, when I was about two years old, I started doing this thing where every night at 2 a.m. I'd wake up crying and asking for oatmeal. What did my mom do? She woke right up and made me that oatmeal. She'd bring me a hot steaming bowl, and I'd look at it and go, "Maple brown sugar?" And if she said no I'd say, "Take it back!"

Mom likes to say that this phase lasted a long time, until I was about seven or maybe fifteen. My main problem with it now is that I didn't demand something a little more filling, like Krispy Kremes or a Big Mac. Also, it does seem like I could've at least said, "Take it back! Please!" Though obviously maple brown sugar oatmeal is the superior oatmeal.

Thanks to my mom—and I think we can all agree that there's a very strong link here—my stomach is so weak and coddled that to this day, I can't even eat in front of TV shows like *ER* and *Cops*. The only show

I can watch while I'm eating is *Seinfeld,* because I know that Jerry will not go "*Newman!*" and then start performing open-heart surgery on his neighbor, no matter how annoying he is. Though now that I think about it, there are even some *Seinfeld*s that are too graphic to watch while I'm eating. You know that one where Poppie pees on the sofa? That's the last thing I need if I'm drinking a Diet Mountain Dew. Just gets my brain thinking too much. Yep. Squeamish about body stuff too.

There is one and only one exception to my skittishness around blood and injuries, and that is watching UFC. It's a pretty big exception because UFC is basically two dudes literally trying to rip each other's heads off. There are non-rubber brains spilling out, non-ketchup blood is smeared on the mat, and if anyone ever goes "*Newman!*" they're screaming it in pain as someone breaks their arm.

But for some reason I like it, and I think it's maybe because they're all wearing gloves. Sure, someone might yank out an eyeball every now and then, but at least they're being clean about it, you know?

Laura woke me up at six in the morning on July 8 to tell me her water broke.

This is probably a good time to tell you that unlike me, my wife is not at all squeamish. Meaning she is basically a barbarian. No joke, one time she got stuck at home in a hurricane, and when I called from the road to see if she was okay, she said, "Are you kidding? What an adventure! Half the block is gone, the wind is howling, and death is raining from the sky! I'm just sad we never lost power!" So to her, giving birth was nothing. By the time she finished giving me the news, she was halfway to the hospital on foot, shouting, "See you there!"

But I totally had the jitters. We were still staying with my parents, so I walked upstairs, knocked on their door, and said, "Mom and Dad, it's time to go." Then I was like, "But you know, we can also just stay here. Pretty sure Laura's got this covered." I could tell my mom was nervous too. Mostly about how she was gonna pay off this crazy bet she'd made with her daughter-in-law.

She goes, "It's okay, son! You got this!" trying to sound all reassuring. But I saw a little twitch in her eye, and I thought, "She ain't talking about the birth! She just wants that million bucks!"

When we got to the delivery room, everyone was wearing gloves, but for some reason it was not comforting like in UFC. In fact, when they made me wear gloves it actually made things worse. They didn't expect me to *touch* anything here, did they? I thought we already discussed this! I am the dad. I am a spectator. I am not a licensed medical professional. I will not be handling any shiny little instruments, I will not be saying, "We need that done, stat!" Keep all fluids and other various parts away from me. If you want to give me grappling gloves and call in Noah Wyle to cut this umbilical cord, be my guest. Otherwise, please leave me out of it.

And honestly, my squeamishness aside, I was really only being logical. I looked around the room, and these guys were *prepared*. They had gone to doctor school. There were machines and tubes and lights and beeps, and these doctors knew exactly how it all worked. They had done this before, at least three or four times. Why would they possibly want my help? What would they get out of it, except maybe a few laughs when I passed out on the floor?

What would I get out of it, except yet another concussion that would make me even dumber than I was in the seventh grade? Would I get a discount on the bill for helping out with the doctor surgery? Would the insurance people be like, "Well, we got a cord-cutter here. Guess this one's a freebie." "Hey, this Nate Bargatze dude was pretty good! Nice, clean snip. Let's see if he's around to perform our next random surgery." When my wife won the bet, she probably wouldn't even share any of her winnings with me, because she controlled all the finances in our house anyway. There was nothing in this entire umbilical business for me. It made no sense!

Laura, for her part, was busy counting every penny of the million bucks she was about to take from my mom. She was also, I guess, giving birth.

If I'm being honest, most of Harper's birth happened in a haze for me. It was like the baby came out and everything was happening so fast. She was big, even I could see that, and she weighed more than eight pounds. When she was born, the umbilical cord was actually wrapped around her neck and she was very blue, but she got a good healthy color as soon as they pulled the cord away, and she was healthy and beautiful and perfect.

I was sobbing, an absolute mess. All I could think of was how amazing our child was, nothing else even crossed my mind, and before I even

Both exhausted from the umbilical cord.

knew what was happening, the good Southern doctor pressed these scissors with these big round blades into my hand and I cut the umbilical cord and that was that. Easy. Like I never had a doubt.

And, of course, I was relieved. Because my mom would not have to un-retire to pay off my wife due to my squeamishness.

Now, I'll be honest. I didn't suddenly become Super Dad right then and there. I didn't stop worrying about stuff or forget about all my squeamishness. If anything, once Harper came into our lives in some ways I actually got worse.

How was this hospital—full of actual baby professionals—letting *me* take this baby home? I didn't have a Dad License. I hadn't taken any classes. What if Harper got pigeon toes? What if she wanted oatmeal in the middle of the night? Could newborns even eat oatmeal? Sure, there were probably books about raising kids out there, but then I'd have to read. Now I was suddenly supposed to have a clue because of, like, nature or something?

Laura and I decided to stay with my parents a few months before heading back to New York, because, you know, maybe they knew something about parenthood. We put Harper's crib in our walk-in closet, just to keep her close. One of our first nights, she started crying something awful. Cried all night, kept crying even when I fed her, even when I burped her. No matter what I tried, she kept crying. I took my bawling daughter to my mom and said, "Mom, I think we gotta take her back."

She said, "Nathan, we are not returning your baby. Trust me, she ain't broken."

When it was time for us to sleep train our girl, I couldn't even stand it. Sleep training is apparently this thing where, to get your baby to start sleeping at regular times, you just let her cry it out. Like scream and holler until she finally falls asleep. Laura told me about this, and I said, "That sounds like torture. For me."

How was I gonna let my little daughter suffer and do nothing about it? Forget about her pain—I'd be miserable! Laura had to wait until I was on the road doing comedy, and then she handled it herself. It was, she claimed, "easy." Because, like I said, she is a barbarian.

In fact, remember that hurricane I told you Laura sat through, bored? She wants me to be clear that that was Hurricane Sandy. It actually happened a few months *after* Harper was born, and Laura, Harper, and Laura's dad braved the hurricane in New York City by themselves, while I was on the road doing comedy. Again. Let the women, children, and elderly fend for themselves, I always say. (There, you happy, Laura? Barbarian!)

But on the day of Harper's birth, for one quick, crazy moment, I really was Super Dad. I was brave. I kept it together. Nothing mattered except my daughter. It was just me and her, and she was gorgeous, and I didn't even notice all the blood and weird, like, fluids everywhere. Though now that I'm thinking about it, it's kinda turning my stomach. And I am realizing just how lucky my mom was that she didn't lose that bet and wind up in the poorhouse.

Laura, for her part, couldn't believe I managed to cut Harper's cord, though she said her attention had been focused on other things. I am still not clear on what those other things were. Thinking about all the money she was gonna win, I guess.

When my mom found out I did it, she just smiled and said, "I told you, I know my son." I guess years of waking up in the middle of the night to feed a crying child instant oatmeal will give you a pretty strong bond. A sticky, paste-like bond flavored with artificial maple and brown sugar. She even let the whole million-dollar-debt thing slide.

Although I am personally waiting for the bill to come due at any moment.

RANDOM FOOD THING 4:
MY PARENTS WAITED IN LINE THREE HOURS FOR WHATABURGER

A few years ago, my parents waited in line for three hours for the grand opening of a fast-food place called Whataburger in our town of Old Hickory. Three hours. After sitting in their car for half the afternoon and moving maybe twenty feet closer to the drive-thru window, my dad turned to my mom and shrugged.

"What else we gonna do?"

Not going with them is the only time in my life I have done anything smarter than a literal clown/magician. Though if I'm being honest, I just happened to be out of town. If I had been around, I probably would've been in the back seat going, "I hear they got this incredible Dr Pepper milkshake. I didn't even know Dr Pepper had milk in it! Let's give it another three hours."

It doesn't take much for folks down South to get excited. Sure, this was the first Whataburger in Tennessee. But it wasn't even the *real* first. We'd already had a few Whataburgers a bunch of years earlier—and they'd all gone out of business. So we went from not even wanting them to basically breaking down the door. That's like me going back to my old job reading water meters and saying, "There was probably a good reason I left. But sometimes I wake up in a cold sweat and wonder, 'What if?'"

Did people care that the brand-new restaurant was actually kinda old? Heck no! Cops were out directing traffic and closing off streets. Helicopters were hovering in the air for no particular reason. The state newspaper covered it like it was some major event. Seriously. So the editor that day said, "Political corruption? Crime? Forget it! I want our best people on that Whataburger opening! I smell a scoop! And also french fries!"

My brother's wife Celesta works in a medical building right behind the restaurant, and no one could get in or out. So you had patients lying on the sidewalk, waiting to get their appendix removed, and shouting at strangers, "Can y'all at least grab me one of those Dr Pepper milkshakes? I hear they're incredible!"

And then people would yell, "Get to the back of the line! You ain't got nothing better to do!"

I mean, there was an actual Burger King, the literal king of burgers, right across the street. *Across the street.* It had zero line. No wait at all. And I know for a fact that my dad loves the Whopper. But no one cared. All the BK employees were probably out waiting for Whataburger too, hoping they could buy a meal and beg for a job: "Please, for once in our lives we want to work at the *cool* fast food place."

People in the South are famous for being polite, but *you* try waiting for three hours on an empty stomach. Drivers started going crazy. Cutting people off, making rude gestures. I believe someone actually honked a horn, which in Tennessee is the same as dropping a nuclear bomb.

My dad was convinced people were cutting in line. He was sure they were sneaking through the Lowe's next door and walking up to the Whataburger without waiting their turn. "That ain't right! That guy wasn't shopping at Lowe's! Do you see a rake? Do you see a screwdriver? I wanna see an arm full of two-by-fours! Build something for me, dadgummit!"

Dadgummit, as you recall, is his favorite swear word.

Half the reason it was taking so long was because everyone was ordering way more than they should. Like, well, I waited so long I might as well stock up. Buy enough to feed the whole family for a week. They'd drive away with bags and bags of burgers and fries and Dr Pepper milkshakes piled up way past the windshield. They could barely even see the road through all this food. My dad would just scream.

"They're backing us all up! Order for the whole line, why don't you! So we can all go home! That ain't right! *It just ain't right!*"

Then he thought about it. And took out his cell phone. "Well. Might as well call around and see if anyone else wants some."

A few minutes after they finally drove away from Whataburger, my dad and mom got to my brother's house. They had enough food for the entire family. There were orders for third cousins and fifth uncles no one ever even heard of. They don't even live in Tennessee. What were they gonna do? Airmail people fries? Maybe a few packets of special sauce?

My parents walked through the door with all this food like conquering heroes, giving off a glow of victory like the Vandy football team after a .500 season. They opened up each greasy bag like it was something sacred. They handed out the burgers like they were passing out holy communion after a preacher's three-hour sermon.

The kids gobbled everything down in a second. They didn't care what it was. They barely even knew it was food. Probably coulda handed them an old shoe covered in Thousand Island. They wouldn't know the difference. They're just kids. They have sense.

But for my dad—for my dad, this was a big deal. The moment of truth.

He pulls out his Whataburger, still slightly warm after their big adventure, and he takes a big ol' bite. Chews. Thinks. Frowns. Mumbles something about "the bun not soaking up the grease quite right." Then he looks up and says all matter-of-fact:

"Burger King is better."

They didn't go back until just a couple months ago, when they drove over so they could send me this photo of where they'd been stuck in line on opening day. Proving they still have nothing better to do.

You can see a tiny "W" far away.
After they took this shot, my dad went and got himself a shake. Zero wait.

I AM DEFINITELY NOT SHOPPING RIGHT NOW

I am definitely not shopping right now. I am walking around.

Yes, I am walking around in a mall. Yes, I have some money in my pocket. Yes, I am going into shops and looking at shop-like things in those shops, and then going into more shops after that. But I am absolutely, 100 percent not shopping right now, even though my wife Laura says this is shopping. I'm pretty sure she doesn't know what she is talking about.

Laura says that the simple act of walking around a mall and maybe—*maybe*—trying on a few things is shopping. That idea is so ridiculous that I just had a hard time typing it. Also, I am bad at typing. Also, I am not actually typing this, because it's a voice memo. Who has time to type while you're definitely *not* shopping? I am walking around. And voice memos are perfect for that. Obviously.

Shopping is not shopping until you buy something, and *then* it is shopping. The buying is the most important part. Laura says, "Shopping is shopping and buying is buying." I say, when a couple fights over shopping, is it from one of them *not* spending money? No, because that's absurd. Because if you fight over shopping, you're really fighting about buying stuff, because *that's* shopping.

Unless, of course, you're fighting about what shopping is or is not, like me and Laura are doing—which, by the way, is definitely also not shopping. Is it walking around? I have no idea, because I stopped understanding what I was saying about five minutes ago.

But I can tell you one thing for sure—I am only walking around right now. I am not shopping.

I just walked up to the checkout counter at this sports shop and set down a box of new Nike shoes that I just tried on. Then I got out my wallet, and I took out my credit card. Then I started to hand my credit card to the lady behind the register. Then, right before she took it from me, I grabbed it back from her and said, "Nope."

Was I ever really going to buy those Nikes? No. But that is exactly the point I am making. Because at no time was that actually shopping. When I *started* to buy, it was *almost* shopping. But as soon as I stopped buying, it became *not* shopping, and went back to being just walking around. It's very simple. It was also probably annoying for the lady behind the register. Which I know it was, because she said, "Hey, this is annoying to me." But it still definitely wasn't shopping.

Laura's like, "If I go to a store to get some shoes, but I try a few things on and decide not to buy anything, are you telling me I did not just go shopping? What exactly was I doing? Shoe-trying-on-with-*maybe*-shopping-but-not-*actually*-shopping?"

And I say "walking-around-and-trying-on-with-maybe-shopping-but-not-actually-shopping" would be the most accurate way to put that. In fact, I bet it's already a word. I will look it up in the dictionary I don't own when I get home from not shopping.

Now I just walked up to the same lady behind the register, and I showed her a nice hat I am definitely not shopping for. Just showed it to her. That's all. Like, "Hey, look at this thing right here." And she said, "Sir, are you gonna buy anything?" and I went, "AHA! Which is why I am *not* shopping!" She said, "I'm gonna get my manager." I said, "Understandable."

When I was growing up, everyone went to malls. That's just what you did to pass the time. Malls were there, and they were big, and they had shops and fast-food places and a few benches and fake plants, so you went there to walk around when you were bored. That's what I use malls for now. They're just a place to go and walk around and look at stuff when I'm bored. If they invent a mall that's not shops, I will be more than happy to go there.

Then Laura says, "Yes, except a mall without shops is by definition not a mall."

To that I say, "Prove it by looking it up in the dictionary we do not own." And you know what? She can't.

Honestly, I would walk around at zoos if I could, except there's not zoos everywhere. If people start building zoos every few blocks, if they make zoos that are easy to get in and out of, I will go to those zoos every single day and I will look at those animals. Is that shopping for animals? No. Even if they put a price tag on the fence in front of the giraffe, I am still just walking around.

Though I probably will stop and look at the price tag, because I'm actually kind of curious how much a giraffe costs. And if that giraffe happens to be wearing shoes and hats that I can look at and maybe also try on, all the better. I'm not making any demands here. I am just saying that I would find a giraffe wearing a cap and matching shoes and socks to be kind of interesting.

But I will not walk out of that zoo with that giraffe, or with the hat and shoes he's hopefully wearing, so I am definitely not shopping right now.

I just finished trying on a dozen different hats, a dozen pairs of shoes, a dozen shirts, and a dozen gym shorts at the sports store. Then I folded and stacked them all directly in front of the lady behind the register and her manager, a large man who was standing next to her with his arms crossed in front of his chest. My stack was a very big stack, like, so big it almost tipped right on top of them. Then I said, "I'm just walking around."

They yelled, "YOU CAN NEVER SHOP HERE AGAIN!"

And I was like, "Exactly. I'll see you tomorrow."

THIS IS TOTALLY OUR YEAR

All right, y'all. I've got a huge prediction to make about Vanderbilt football. Huge. You ready for it? Okay then.

We are going to be undefeated this year. Whenever you are reading this. No matter the year. If it's the middle of the season and Vandy has a loss already, then I am talking about the next year. Because this is how I feel before every season.

If such a bold prediction makes you nervous, I understand. I'm not trying to jinx us. So instead of focusing on the whole undefeated thing, let's just say we will definitely make a bowl game, and we will also definitely win that bowl game. The Commodores* probably won't make the national championship, I'll give you that. But honestly, no—I won't give you that. I think there's a good chance that we absolutely will 100 percent win the national championship this year. And that counts from now until the end of time.

---

* The founder of Vanderbilt, Cornelius Vanderbilt, was known as "the Commodore" because he started out in the steamboat business. So Vandy is called the Commodores. And I am such a big fan I didn't even have to look that up. Maybe.

Now, I know what you guys are thinking. You're thinking, "Nate, everyone knows that the 'Dores* traditionally stink at football. We've usually got a better shot of losing all our games than winning any of them. We don't regularly go to bowl games. And we will never win the national championship." (Side note: We *have* won national championships in baseball and women's bowling. We are a problem in women's bowling. Your problem.)

You may also be thinking, "Hey wait a minute, isn't this a book? I could be reading this five years after you wrote it. There's no way you know a thing about Vandy's chances this season!"

All I can say is that I got a feeling. A good feeling. A very good, very strong feeling that we will go undefeated this year. And if you don't understand why I have to believe that—why I *need* to believe that, no matter what—then you do not understand what it feels like to be a loser.

I do, however, understand what it feels like, because I am a Vandy fan. I will always be a Vandy fan, no matter how much we lose. Or maybe because of it.

Sometimes I'm not sure which.

I am such a big Vandy fan that people actually think I went to Vandy. This is not a joke. Even people who *went to Vandy*—so these are smart people!—think I went to Vandy. As if I seriously *attended* the university.

On the one hand, okay. I talk about the 'Dores constantly. I obsess over them in a very public way, and this is not a school that normal sports fans obsess over, because, well, they are Vandy. That's like someone who's really into fast food obsessing over Jack in the Box. They ain't McDonald's. They ain't Chick-fil-A. You don't love them, you don't hate them, everyone is basically fine with them, and that's that. Not me. I am a die-hard fan of everything Commodores. Including our women's bowling team, which really is very excellent.

---

* This is short for "Commodores." But you knew that. Because everyone knows.

On the other hand, come on—me, go to Vanderbilt? It is public knowledge that I am not good at school. I have built my entire career as a comic on the documented fact that I barely, just *barely* made it out of high school. So I am *horrible* at school, and pretty much the entire world knows it. Vandy, however, is a school for brains. I mean these are some of the world's top intellectual minds in the field of solving stuff and things and whatever else. Obviously I couldn't get into Vandy.

But Vandy alum do not care about this monumental difference in our respective mental abilities. They still claim me as one of their own. They give me great seats for the games. They even let me come and talk to the football team. And I'll say things that I think are motivational and sportsy. Like, "Hey, come on now." Or "I guess you gotta just hit that ball out there pretty good, all right?"

The players look at each other and shrug.

"Did someone say this dude actually went here?"

"Shut up! He likes us! Leave him alone!"

They're both grateful and totally confused—not only because I love Vandy, but because I *choose* to love Vandy. If I didn't go to school there, why be a fan? Why spend so much time and energy on a sports team that never wins? Why not pick Tennessee, which is the team most of my friends cheer for? I mean, the Vols don't always win, but they're not losers. They've got a huge stadium, and flashy orange colors, and Peyton Manning, and all these traditions they're proud of, like not being horrible.

Heck, why not obsess over a pro team like the Titans? Why not pee-wee football? Why not *anything*? Pick a competitive knitting league! Walk into a concrete wall over and over and over again! Choose any one of those things and they will be more rewarding than being a Vandy football fan. So why?

Some of that comes down to roots, our family history. My town of Old Hickory is about a thirty-minute drive from the Vanderbilt campus. My cousin Ronnie Bargatze, who really took my dad under his wing when he first came to Nashville, used to be an assistant coach for Vandy's basketball team, and then he went on to be a color commentator on the local radio station for Vandy basketball games. My mom used to work at Vanderbilt in the ticket office. Back when I was a kid, my dad took me to every single Vandy football game, and lots of Vandy basketball games too. Yes, we lost almost all of them.

For a few years as a boy, my younger brother Derek actually abandoned Vandy to root for Tennessee, which also happens to be our biggest rival. This betrayal was on the same level as Benedict Arnold, and whatever he did in that one war, except that my brother's had real consequences. He wore an orange UT sweatsuit almost every day, and he even painted the walls of his bedroom a bright and cheerful orange. All because Derek wanted to cheer for a team that, and I quote, "won games" and "actually had something to celebrate." Also because he's a bad person.

My family could not take this lack of loyalty to our adopted lost cause. We refused to even go into Derek's orange room, which he probably did not mind. But then my parents decided to cut off his entire supply of merch, and really anything orange. No hats, no shirts, no koozies. No orange Kool-Aid, no actual oranges. No sunsets, no sunrises. Basically, no joy of any sort was allowed. Only Vandy's noble but gloomy black with metallic gold trim. And Vandy merch, which was also pretty limited because no one sells Vandy merch, because no one likes Vandy. Sometime during high school my brother finally caved to all the pressure. Now he is a Vandy fan, happy being miserable with the rest of us. As God intended.

So yeah. In the South, we take our bond with our team seriously. I mean, I know people take their team seriously all over the place, but especially in the South. It's not just your team, it's your tribe, it's your heritage, it's who you give your allegiance to.

In 2008, the 'Dores actually went to a bowl game. I mean, it was the Music City Bowl, played in Nashville, so this wasn't exactly the Orange

Bowl or anything, but still—this was our first bowl game since way back in 1982, when I was three years old.

My mom didn't work in the ticket office anymore, but her friend Debbie did, and Debbie got me a ticket. I was so excited, I got to the stadium two and a half hours early to pick it up before tailgating with my friends. Except instead of just handing me my ticket so I could use it later, Debbie tore it right then and there. What was I gonna do? Tell this close friend of the family that she made a mistake? Ask for *another* free ticket?

So I had no choice—I had to go take my seat hours before the game started.

This was December 31. It was freezing cold. Nothing was open yet. I couldn't get a hot dog, I couldn't get hot chocolate, I couldn't ask a vendor to breathe warm air on my frozen hands. It was just me, sitting by myself, waiting for my friends, who probably figured I had died a martyr of my Vandy fanhood, the only person in the stands in a stadium that holds sixty-seven thousand people, staring like an idiot at a hundred yards of empty turf.

And it. Was. Awesome.

Because I was first, man! Can you imagine any bigger sign of loyalty than that? Sitting in a deserted stadium waiting for hours to watch your team play its first bowl game in over twenty-five years. We even won the game. Our punter was the MVP of the game. It doesn't get more Vandy than that.

Of course, the next year we hit a little bump in the road. Won two games all year, lost ten.

But that's the other part of being a Vandy fan. It's not just shared history, it's not just loyalty to a place or a school that you didn't actually attend—it's about rooting for the underdog.

There's something special about cheering for a team that constantly loses. You gotta be strong. You gotta be resilient. Most importantly, you have to be a little crazy. Supporting a loser isn't usually fun. It definitely isn't uplifting. But it *is* different. It takes heart. It takes dedication. You're David, always striving against Goliath. You get to be rebellious. You get to cut against the grain. You get to take pride in those few miraculous victories you can actually claim as your own.

I mean, seriously, what's even the point of being a Tennessee fan? (I'd ask my friends, but I refuse to give them the satisfaction.) You win a few games, you lose a few less. That's nice, I guess. That exists. I can't even imagine being a Georgia or Alabama fan. What is that, just one constant party, all year long? Who wants that? All that cheering and noise and laughter and happiness. That would just give me a headache. No thank you, ma'am.

Being a fan of those teams asks nothing of you. Anyone can be a fan, and everyone is. It's simple. It's easy. How boring.

My wife and I got married on Friday the 13th. Some of that was because we are both cheap, though for the record she's the cheaper one. I mean, how easy is it to rent out a wedding venue on Friday the 13th? We just called 'em up and they said, "Sure, you don't even need a reservation. Just come on by the day of. You'll have the place all to yourself."

But some of it was because this was a Friday the 13th in October—and Vandy had a football game on Saturday, which I obviously didn't want to miss. We were playing Georgia, and, in case you somehow missed it, Georgia is very, very good at football. Annoyingly good.

So you're probably wondering, "Nate, why would you possibly organize your wedding date around a game that Vandy was guaranteed to lose?"

Well, guess what, smart guy. We won that game. Go ahead, look it up. Vandy versus Georgia, October 14, 2006. Beat the Bulldogs 24–22, on a last-second field goal. It was a miracle, and Laura and I have always been able to say that we have the luckiest marriage on the planet. And you know what? We do.

Now, what if we were Tennessee fans? And what if that had been Tennessee beating Georgia that Saturday instead of Vandy? That would've been cool, sure. Maybe a mild upset. Always swell to win a football game. But would it have meant as much? Of course not. We would've been pleased for a while, and then we would've gone about our day, and now we'd be divorced, and it would be all Tennessee's fault.

I also wanna point out that last year on October 5, our unranked football team not only beat Alabama but did it when the Crimson Tide were ranked first in the nation. It was probably the biggest upset in the history of our program, and definitely one of the biggest in the history of college football. After we won the game, 40–35, our fans stormed the field, tore down the goalposts, carried them through Nashville, and tossed them in the Cumberland River.

Later that night, I hosted *Saturday Night Live* for the second time. Coincidence? I don't think so. My only regret is that me and Laura didn't renew our vows after the show.

I may not have gone to Vanderbilt, but I did attend one year of community college. The fact that I did not attend any more years after that one year should tell you something.*

The only class in community college I came even close to enjoying was my remedial speech class. It turns out I can speak. I know—that surprised me too. It was the fall of 1997, and the teacher wanted me to give a presentation about something I really loved. I think you can tell where this is going.

Turns out that Vandy had just opened the season going 2–1. Now, two wins and one loss might not sound that great to you, but that just tells me you *still* don't get what it means to be a Vandy fan. I was absolutely convinced we would make a bowl game that year. I just knew, in my heart of hearts, that we were going to win like we'd never won before. That this was finally—*finally*—gonna be our year.

---

*As you recall, after community college I then flunked out of Western Kentucky after a semester. Zero credits.

I got so excited, I did something I'd never done before. I actually prepared for a class.

That's right. I decided that I was going to do a whole speech about the greatness of Vandy football. I had all my arguments ready about how we were all set to dominate. I knew our stats, I knew all our players at every single position. I even put together a Vandy highlight reel to use as a visual aid. Keep in mind that this was years before digital video became a thing. How the heck an idiot like me managed to put together a VHS highlight reel is something I do not comprehend even to this day. But the honor of Vandy football required it of me, so I did it. Gladly.

I got up there in front of that classroom full of Tennessee fans—this was when Peyton was the quarterback, so *everyone* loved the Vols—and I gave the most passionate, most fiery, most hilariously out-of-touch speech you can possibly imagine about Vandy football. The other students loved it. They all laughed so hard, I think with me, but I'm still not sure. And I got my first and only A on a college assignment.

Vandy went on to lose almost every other game they played that season. Ended up going 3–8 overall. Didn't even come close to making a bowl game. And I didn't get any college credits for the speech class. They told me it was because it was a remedial course, so it didn't count for anything, but it was probably because the teacher was a Tennessee fan.

That's all right though. We're gonna beat those guys this year.

I have a very good feeling.

TAKE ANOTHER BREATH.
YOU'RE WELCOME.

I BELIEVE IN ELVES

I want to start by saying that if you are a young child reading this book, and you believe in the Christmas Elf, then the Christmas Elf is absolutely, positively, 100 percent real, and also you should skip this chapter and go on to the next one.

Not for any reason. Just because.

Actually, if you're a grown adult who happens to still believe in the Christmas Elf, then you should also skip to the next chapter, and I want you to know that not only is the Christmas Elf totally real, but I also do not judge you and your older elf beliefs in any way.

Because the fact is that the Christmas Elf is extremely neat.* For those of you who don't know—and I know you're out there, and I truly feel sorry for you—here is the basic deal with the Christmas Elf: This little dude visits your house every night of December before Christmas. He always hides somewhere fun and silly, so the kids have to find him in the morning before he reports back to Santa on their behavior during

---

*I am aware that maybe most people call it "Elf on the Shelf." I think we should also call it Elf on the Shelf, but for some reason we started calling it Christmas Elf.

the day. I've been told that there are other ways to do the Christmas Elf tradition, but this is the way our family does it, so obviously it is the correct way.

Sure, Santa is the one who gets all the press. The catchy tunes, the cookies and milk, the picture on all the Coke ads. I mean, who knows how much this guy is collecting in royalties each year. But think about it. If you're a kid, you're lucky if you're seeing Santa once after waiting for an hour in a jam-packed mall. You get in, he says *ho-ho-ho*, they shove a little broken candy cane into your hand, and it's over. Done. All you can do is hope you made a decent impression on this large stranger who holds the fate of your entire Christmas in his pudgy, mittened hand.

But the Christmas Elf—that's the one you're forming the relationship with. He is in your house. You see him every day, you talk to him, you share personal information, you make eye contact. Yeah, he plays a little hard to get, but it's more fun that way. You are bonding with that Elf. That Elf is your buddy. And until a few months ago, he was my daughter's buddy as well.

Last chance, kids!

Just move along to the next chapter. Nothing to see here. Nothing. At. All.

Okay!

For those of you still here, you should know that my daughter Harper was eleven years old when this happened. Now, you might be thinking that sounds a little old to still be believing in something like a Christmas Elf. And I might be thinking that you have a heart made of coal, and that Santa definitely will not be leaving anything in your stocking this year.

My daughter and I are very close. My wife sometimes reminds me that I need to be Harper's dad, a guy who can provide discipline and wisdom, and I shouldn't think of Harper as my friend. This, of course, is ridiculous. Harper is not my friend. She is my *best* friend.

As close as we are though, my job means I spend a lot of time on the road traveling, away from my family. Harper loves to travel too. When she was younger she'd pack her Minnie Mouse suitcase full of her stuffies and she loved staying in hotels, and once when she saw that I was about to leave with my suitcase, she grabbed hers and said, "Can I come too?" and I pretty much died. I still talk to her on the phone every single day. But some of those conversations are her going, "Hey Dad, I'm busy talking to my friend Katie. Bye." Then she hangs up on me and I think, "Fine—now you are my *second*-best friend. After your mother." Who, by the way, is also usually busy when I call.

But no matter what, the one thing Harper and I have always had is Christmas and the Elf. I would go all out for that thing, man. I mean, so creative! There was one time when I hid the Elf in the refrigerator, and I was like, the Elf is cold, so I put a little towel on it as a blanket. Then there was another time I thought I'd put it in the bath, except then it would get wet, so I was like, instead of water I'll use . . . marshmallows! Wow, that was a good one. Anyway, eventually I just bought a kit, because honestly it really is hard thinking of all that stuff.

There were times when I had to be on the road even during December, and my dad would take over Elf duty for those nights. He would just go crazy. He did a thing where he pretended the Christmas Elf was flying through the air, so he dangled it from a whole bunch of balloons, and then there was fake snow falling from the ceiling, and Harper absolutely loved it, like I never heard the end of just how great the flying Christmas Elf was while Daddy was gone.

Which, now that I think about it, that was really unfair. I mean, my father is a trained, professional magician. This is a man who was on a first-name basis with the Easter Bunny! Granted, it was actually a dude who dressed up as the Easter Bunny and carpooled with my dad to children's shows, but still—how was I supposed to compete with that?

You take any holiday—I'm talking Halloween, I'm talking Thanksgiving, Labor Day, Presidents' Day, whatever—and my dad will find a way to make it more fun. You want a turkey that'll guess what card you're holding while trying to bust its way out of a straitjacket? He will make that happen. Actually, he will make that happen even if you do not want it. And yes, it will get awkward for both you and the bird.

Harper got so into our Christmas Elf that she actually gave him his own name—Alfie. I'm pretty sure it started out as "Elfie," but then at some point she turned that into Alfie, probably because she's a genius. She started writing these long letters to Alfie and leaving them on the kitchen counter for him every night, asking him questions about her presents and life in the North Pole and whether he'd be able to keep visiting after Christmas was over and stay with her forever.

If that doesn't make you sob with emotion, then maybe you'll cry when you find out I was in charge of writing her back. I mean, look—I did the best I could. I'd write his replies using my left hand, so at least Alfie seemed to have his own awkward, elf-style handwriting. But it also quickly became clear that Alfie had no idea how to spell even basic English. Maybe because *I* have no idea how to spell even basic English.

I know—you're sitting there right now thinking, "Dude, I'm reading this *whole book* you wrote, and the spelling seems fine to me." All right, smart guy—have you never heard of this thing called a copyeditor? You think the publisher would put out a book where their author can't even spell the word "author"? Which, by the way, I just needed autocorrect for. Twice.

But Alfie didn't have a copyeditor. Alfie didn't have autocorrect. Alfie just had my hooked left hand trying to figure out if it's "presents" or "presence" or maybe "presense," and admitting that he wasn't exactly sure where the North Pole is, but possibly someplace up.

So Harper never thought Alfie was very sharp. But she didn't care. She loved him anyway. She loved writing to him, even when his answers made no sense. She loved searching for him, even when his hiding places were about as inventive as "on the floor." Or one of our favorites, "same place as last night." She loved Alfie, and she believed in him.

And I figured she would keep believing in him, you know, forever. High school—not even a question. College—I could sneak into her dorm room at nights and plant Alfie behind her backpack, I'm sure her roommates won't mind. And when she got married and had kids of her own—even better, because I could just coordinate with the rest of her family. Me, her husband, and my grandkids, keeping the Legend of Alfie the Christmas Elf alive for my daughter. She never had to know.

Then, a couple years ago, right after Christmas, Harper finally found out.

Let me tell you, it was bad.

I was already on the alert, because a few days after the Elf's final visit, I had successfully quashed what I thought would be the biggest threat to our Christmas spirit.

For reasons I cannot comprehend, my wife cannot throw away a box. This is a thing she just cannot do. It's as if, in her mind, our house is right on the brink of a devastating box shortage. This is strange, because we are getting about twenty boxes delivered to us every day. Everything comes now in its own individual box. I ordered a hundred toothpicks, and Amazon delivered each one in its own box, and each box was as big as my head. So why on earth do we need to save all these boxes?

She'll be like, "Well, what if we need to move?"

I'll go, "Why would we need to move?"

"Because," she says, "I'm running out of space for all these boxes!"

So our garage is full of boxes, and no one ever goes there, because why would you. Except a couple days after Christmas it snowed, so my daughter went in there to get her sled. And I walked outside so we could go sledding together, and she's standing there with the box that her bike had come in. Her bike which I had assembled the day *before* Christmas and placed under the tree with a big bow as a present from Santa.

And she goes, "Dad, is this where my bike came from?"

Most men, when confronted with the collapse of their daughter's beliefs, would panic. Thankfully, I'm good at thinking on my feet. So I go, "I don't know what it is! Your mom just keeps all these dumb boxes everywhere!"

Once Harper was distracted by all the dumb boxes, I grabbed the sled and hurried her out of the garage. Then after we got back I just hid the bike box under all the other dumb boxes, and it is probably there to this day. Crisis averted, Christmas saved forever. Yay me.

But then a couple weeks later, the weather got nice, so I went outside to exercise.

And you know what, let me just take a step back here and say that absolutely nothing good ever comes of exercising. I mean, if I had just been inside, watching TV, and letting my health decline like usual, none of this would've happened. But no. I just had to do a squat, didn't I? For that, I sacrificed my precious daughter's magical innocence.

Anyway, I was right in the middle of a crunch or a press or something that involved way too much grunting, when suddenly my wife Laura ran outside.

"You gotta get in here!" she shouted. "Harper was on YouTube and she saw a thing about how to hide your Christmas Elf, and she's flipping out!"

And you know what, let me just take another step back here and say that absolutely nothing good ever comes from the internet. Or really technology in general. We only let our daughter watch YouTube Kids. Let me repeat that: YouTube. Kids. Why would something that's only for children show a video that basically tells them their Christmas Elf isn't real? What other dreams are we trying to crush today? "Sorry, kid, but you got 'boring desk job' written all over you. Yep, you can forget that whole astronaut thing."

So I go inside, and Laura is right. Our daughter is pretty much flipping out. Crying, screaming into pillows, going on and on about Alfie and Santa and Christmas all being fake. It was awful. So naturally I look at my wife, and I say, "Doesn't this seem like a mom situation?"

Laura goes, "You're the one who wants to be her best friend."

That was a low blow, and I officially dropped my wife down to fourth- or fifth-best friend, somewhere below my trainer/barber Eric, who you will meet in the next chapter, and who would never say something like that.

I turn to Harper and I say, "Listen, honey, I know this is tough, but you've found out about other things, and it wasn't that big of a deal, right? What about the tooth fairy? You know she's not real."

My daughter says, "Yeah, but that was obvious, because putting an old tooth under your pillow is creepy."

Well, she had me there.

We call up my dad, and he tries explaining to her the real origins of Kris Kringle and giving gifts on Christmas, and it's all very well-intentioned, but Harper is still sobbing, and I'm thinking, "Guess that whole magician thing isn't helping now, is it? Why don't you try attaching some balloons and some fake snow and see what that does for your presentation?"

So we get off the phone and I go, "Look, Harper, this all came from a place of love, all right? I wasn't trying to trick you or make you feel stupid. It's like when we go to Disney World and you see Mickey Mouse or Cinderella. You know it's not the real them, but that's okay. It's just for fun. It's fun to pretend."

It was like something clicked. She slowly stopped crying and after a little while she was okay. I figured, all right, maybe being a part of my little girl's life isn't just about holidays and presents and elves. Even though that is a very fun part of her life. Maybe I gotta start working on just talking to her, communicating with her, as her friend and her dad. Just as long as I don't gotta write her any notes.

After Harper settled down, we talked about how next Christmas maybe she and I could hide Alfie together. How we wouldn't tell her younger cousins, because we wanted them to enjoy the magic of the holiday the same way she did. How that could be our newest tradition, and we could do it just the two of us. She'd hide it one night, and I'd hide it the next.

And you know what? That's exactly what we do, to this day.

MY BARBER MAKES ME WORK OUT

I work very hard to get in shape, which is something I will do either next week or probably never, so I decided to have a trainer who is also my barber. It just makes sense.

This all started because I like my barber Eric. Like, a lot. I mean, it's not weird or anything. He's just a cool guy, and I enjoy hanging out with him. Talking to him about sports. The weather. Life and love. All right, so maybe it's a little weird.

But let's be honest. This is how it is for most dudes and their barbers. Cutting a man's hair is not very complex. You basically say, "Please trim my already-short hair and beard," and that's that. It is true that my chin whiskers grow kind of fast, but even that requires only slightly advanced grooming. So a guy sticks with his barber mostly because they like hanging out. This is an ancient, sacred connection I call the man-barber bond.

If that sounds at all profound to you, you got it exactly backward. The whole point of the man-barber bond is that this is a dude you can be dumb around. You don't talk about anything important or even all that interesting. Heck, half the time you don't even talk. But think about it—how many guys out there could have their hands in your hair, and you'd go, "That's cool. Let's be quiet for a while." And it ain't awkward. It ain't weird. It's just cutting hair. That, my friends, is a very rare thing to find. That is the man-barber bond, and it has been around all of time. I mean, I know nothing about history, but I have played George Washington on TV, and I can tell you he loved his barber. How else do you explain the ponytail?

My man-barber bond with Eric is especially strong because Eric was my Covid Barber. Y'all remember what it was like back then. Barber shops everywhere got shut down, so setting up a haircut became a very delicate matter. Two dudes had to show real trust in each other. You had to be vulnerable. Sensitive. I mean, I've obviously never watched a rom-com, because I only watch the movie *Jack Reacher* over and over, but me asking Eric to be my Covid Barber probably sounded something like a meet-cute:

Me, standing there all awkward, looking at the ground, my hands in my pockets: "Hey . . . uh . . . you wanna come over to my place sometime? Maybe, like, cut my hair?"

Eric, his eyes lighting up, trying but totally failing to hide his excitement: "Are you kidding? I thought you'd never ask!"

Me, way too eager: "Cool. You ain't sick, right?"

Eric, totally clueless: "Of course not! I think."

Me, even more clueless: "Same here! I think."

And if you're gonna point out that I was talking to Eric on the phone and the two of us had already met, so this was literally nothing like a meet-cute, then I will say you're not a fun person.

So anyway, Eric came over to my place, he cut my hair in my garage, which was probably illegal, and after he was done I walked down my driveway and shouted to all my neighbors, "Hey everybody! Free Covid haircuts for the whole neighborhood!"

Five or six guys sprinted over—these shaggy, ragged Grizzly Adams dudes who hadn't gotten trims in months—and suddenly I was running a barbershop speakeasy. Someone started blasting bad jazz—not that I even know what jazz is—and I was seriously about to start handing out glasses of bootleg gin, maybe make a little cash on the side. Then one dude coughed, and it was like Eliot Ness busted down the door for a raid.

Everyone ran for the hills, shirts pulled over their faces. Like, "Thanks for the trim!"

A little while after that, I started having another problem that at first seemed totally different from my hair. This problem was with my clothes.

I'd been doing my usual appearances on TV shows when I began realizing my weight was getting a little high. This was nothing new, necessarily. I'd spent my whole life going through short periods when I was more or less in shape, and much longer periods when all I did was eat Sour Patch Kids in bed. But this time was worse than usual. Before I'd go on camera, I'd look at myself in the mirror and—no joke—you could see my nipples practically blasting through my shirt.

So, like I said. A problem with my clothes.

Even though Eric was just my barber, I knew he was kind of into health stuff. Like every now and then he'd throw out weird terms like "calories" and "exercise." I mean out of *nowhere*. We'd be talking all casual about golf, and suddenly he'd shout, "Body mass index!"

Wisely, I chose to ignore him. But then I also started noticing that physically he was transforming. When I first met him he was maybe a little thick. I'm not saying he was "worry about your nipples" thick, but still—a little thick. Now, though, Eric had become what I always wanted to be myself—which was flat. Simply, perfectly flat. He didn't have any rolls or curves. His body didn't have any hills or valleys or strange detours. He didn't have to worry about how his shirt fit or how his jeans fit. He maybe didn't even have nipples. He was a walking plywood board. Nothing but flat from head to toe. This was what I wanted. Flatness.

Also, he listened to more Joe Rogan than me. That's about as good as a degree from Trainer University, right? So I thought, "What the heck, maybe my barber should be my trainer?" The next time I sat down for a trim, I decided to go for it. In case you were wondering, asking a man who cuts your hair to suddenly take an interest in the shape of your body is about as not-awkward as inviting him over for a trim during a disease:

Me, sitting there all awkward, looking down at my bib: "Hey . . . uh . . . you wanna help me, like, work out and stuff?"

Eric, his eyes lighting up, trying but totally failing to hide his excitement: "Are you kidding? I thought you'd never ask!"

Me, way too eager: "Cool. You listen to Joe Rogan, right?"

Eric, totally clueless: "Yes! That is my only qualification."

Me, even more clueless: "Perfect."

So a couple years ago, Eric became my full-time barber-trainer. He started helping me out at home and he even traveled with me to my shows. He showed me how to exercise and guided me on eating the right foods. He became my personal guru on both health and hair.

And, well, we ran into a little problem. I mean, I'd tried using trainers before, and I was aware that they are not the most fun people. How could they be? Their whole point is to make you exercise, and exercise stinks. This is the job we literally hire them for, but somehow that only makes it more annoying. My old trainer would tell me to do ten squats, and I'd look at him like, "*You* do ten squats. *Golly, what am I paying you for?* In fact, I'm feeling extra motivated today, so toss in a few push-ups while you're at it."

But I figured Eric would be different. He wasn't only cool, he was *barber* cool. This was a guy I could sit around and literally talk about nothing with, and we were happy. We had a bond, an ancient bond, forged by Moses and Caesar and Gandhi and other men with bold haircuts. Working out with Eric would *have to* be fun! I could spin around on his chair—that was exercise, right? When I started to sweat, he could brush me off with one of those little brushes. And that barber pole would have to be good for a chin-up or two. Besides, if I didn't feel like working out, I could just ask for a haircut, and I'd still feel like I was making progress. I might end up bald, but my scalp would definitely feel pretty flat. What could go wrong?

Basically everything, it turns out. Suddenly my barber wasn't only not-cool—he was *trainer* not-cool. Don't get me wrong. It wasn't that Eric was bad at the diet-and-exercise stuff. The problem was he was *great* at it. I told him my goal was to get flat, and he said, "*Flat?* You realize that's not even a thing, right? I want you to be healthy in a lasting, sustainable way."

We'd be in the middle of a haircut, and he'd start going on and on about "calories in/calories out." I'd ask him to trim my beard, and he'd show me the yearlong hundred-step exercise program he'd developed. There were times I didn't even need a haircut, I just wanted that old man-barber bond back, so I'd put on a bib, sit in a chair, and try to talk about the weather—and this dude would order me to do twenty squats. I had my old trainer for that, and he told me to do half as many!

See? There is nothing as not-cool as trainer not-cool. George Washington and Moses and Caesar and Gandhi all hated their trainers. I guarantee you.

It's not that I'm opposed to exercising. I just need to think about exercise in a certain way. If you come to me with some big lifelong master plan that involves keeping track of my diet, maybe jogging once a week at a reasonable pace, doing some light weights to maintain my strength, possibly some work with resistance bands—I'm sorry, dude, but you lost me. Honestly, I started falling asleep in the middle of writing that, that's how dull it was.

I need action. I need excitement. I need all or nothing. Which means I go 100 percent *all in* on buying every dumb gimmick and signing up for every ridiculous health fad—and then I do nothing. It is a foolproof lifelong strategy that has been very great at making me feel very bad. And I wanted to stick with it, thank you very much.

But instead of letting me enjoy my usual self-defeating habits, Eric actually expected me to change and be, like, better.

He'd go, "If you ate nothing but salad with chicken breast every day, you would feel great for the rest of your life," and I'd be like, "I just saw a weeklong cleanse on the internet, where if you click on a pop-up window and eat nothing but lemon juice, allspice, and tabasco sauce, you'll lose seventy pounds and your teeth will fall out. It only costs a thousand bucks!"

He'd go, "Let's start slow with some exercises to increase your core strength," and I'd be like, "I just saw this workout machine that was designed by the Navy SEALs that will put on thirty pounds of muscle in your quads, forty pounds of muscle in your lats, and make you storm the shores of France in a wetsuit. It only costs a thousand bucks!"

He'd go, "Let's try running two miles at a sensible pace," and I'd be like, "I just signed up for an ultramarathon in Nashville in October." That is actually not a joke. I really did sign up for the fifty-mile ultramarathon in Nashville last October. The longest I had ever gone before that was eight miles spread out over thirty-five days.

Thankfully it ended up getting canceled. The bribe I paid the organizer only cost a thousand bucks.

Over the years, I have developed many complicated strategies for avoiding exercise. The main one is not doing exercise.

For example, me and Eric will schedule a time to meet up and work out, and at the last second I'll remember I have something important I have to do, like go to McDonald's, and I'll cancel. Or we'll meet up at the gym, and as soon as I walk through the door I'll pretend to pull a muscle, so maybe we should take a break and go eat McDonald's. Or I won't contact him at all for a few weeks. Is McDonald's involved? I will let you be the judge. Also, yes it is.

But Eric has his strategies too. He's a very clever barber-trainer. He has all these powerful motivational quotes. And he'll text them to me. Every. Single. Day.

Stuff like:

"Don't wait for stress to go down before working on yourself. Work on yourself to make the stress go down."

And:

"Never avoid a personal tune-up on your bodily engine. Because the road is long, but it's better than driving in circles."

And:

"The wise man learns to balance his calorie budget as he learns to balance his financial budget. This is how you'll begin to thrive."

And:

"Hello? Nate?"

And:

"Hello???"

And:

"You know how I said I thought you'd never ask? I lied! I KNEW you'd ask!"

And:

"Bro, you KNOW how crazy your chin whiskers can be!"

And:

"WHATEVER HAPPENED TO GETTING FLAT???"

I do get back to Eric. Eventually.

That's the thing about him. No matter how annoying I am, he never gives up on me. He might not let me get away with my craziest fitness ideas, but at this point he just wants to get me moving. If I feel like doing the treadmill for a few minutes, he'll say cool. If I'd rather spend a couple hours trying to toss a football in a trash can, he'll say, "Well, that's still exercise." Or when we go to McDonald's, we'll stand in front of the menu, and I'll point at something like the Big Mac and go, "Can I eat that?" And he'll say, "What do you think?"

Eventually I'll just order a Diet Coke. Then we'll sit down, and we'll chat about sports. The weather. Life and love. Or maybe we won't say anything at all.

At this rate, I figure I'll be flat by the time you're reading this book. Or at least I'll have a smooth chin and a very nice haircut.

RANDOM FOOD THING 5:
I BETTER TALK THIS OVER WITH MY WIFE

I have no idea what to do with this menu.

I mean, I've been working all morning. On what, I don't know. But whatever it is, it's been very draining and I am absolutely starving for lunch right now.

Then I get to this restaurant, and they want me to what—make a choice about what I'm supposed to eat? I mean, it takes me twenty minutes just to choose a pair of socks on a good day. Now this place wants me to decide what to put in my body—my own body, into my mouth—from twenty different options while I'm in this weakened, hungry condition? And that doesn't even include all the various sauce combinations! Which I believe are three.

All right, Nate. Take a deep breath. Let's just get out the phone and . . .

[*Ring . . . Ring . . .*]
LAURA: Hello?
NATE: Hey.

LAURA: Nate, I'm out at Target shopping with Amanda right now, and we're right in the middle of trying different—

NATE: Is chicken good for you?

LAURA: What?

NATE: Like, if I have a choice here between chicken or ham or beef or turkey, which one do you think is healthy for me? It's chicken, right? Or is that pretty much the same as turkey? I mean, they're both a bird.

LAURA: [*sighs*] Here we go. [*muffled*] Amanda! Amanda, this is gonna be a while. Yeah. Nate's trying to order something to eat. Uh-huh. I'll catch up.

NATE: Hello?

LAURA: Yeah, Nate, I guess if you're talking about those four options, I guess chicken is the one that's good for you. And yes, turkey is definitely also a chicken-like bird.

NATE: Because there's no way I'm doing vegetarian. I gotta put something in my stomach other than lettuce. And turkey obviously feels like a Thanksgiving meat.

LAURA: Obviously. So chicken it is. All right then—

NATE: And I can't do a chicken salad. I did one of those yesterday, and they snuck onions in it, and now I'll never trust chicken salad ever again in my life. So it's definitely gonna be a sandwich. Then I could go simple with some mustard, probably not too spicy, or I might try barbecue sauce. I could actually do something spicy for that, but—

LAURA: Okay, I can't believe I'm making this conversation any longer—but you should really think about that bread. You know you've been trying to cut down on carbs.

NATE: Well, a salad would take us right back to square one.

LAURA: *No!* No, I'm not saying it has to be a salad, Nate. We don't need square one. Just—if you have to do bread, try to do

something that's a little better for you, all right? Do a wheat or
a whole grain or even a wrap.

NATE: A wrap! Come on. That's not even real bread!

LAURA: Nate, I really have to get back to Amanda, all right? Get
a grilled chicken sandwich, make sure the bread is wheat, do
your barbecue sauce, it should probably be mild—

NATE: How about *fried* chicken? Is it okay if the chicken is
fried?

LAURA: No, *grilled* chicken. Grilled chicken sandwich.

NATE: But if I do *no* bread with the fried chicken, isn't that the
same as eating grilled chicken *with* the bread?

[*Sound of phone hanging up.*]

NATE: Laura? Laura?

Well. That seemed a little unreasonable.

I mean, they're coming out with new studies on food all the time.
First eggs are good for you. Then they're bad for you. Then they're good
for you again. Why wouldn't fried chicken without bread be just as
healthy as grilled chicken with bread? I bet there's at least one study
backing me up. That seems like something Laura should know.

I call Laura about stuff at least three or four times a day. Every day.
That doesn't mean text. That means calling. Talking. Discussing. The
old-fashioned way. By cell phone.

This drives Laura crazy. I believe it's because in many ways she's got a
dude brain, and I've got a chick brain. I, for example, like to talk things
out. What I will have for lunch. What shirt I will wear today. Whether
ranch counts as a dressing or sauce. So basically all things. And I hate to
mow the lawn, which also feels like a chick-brain thing. Laura, on the
other hand, hates to talk about pretty much everything except our feel-
ings. Which are gross, and who wants to talk about that? She also likes
to mow the lawn, which makes no sense to anyone.

Is it my fault she's got a dude brain? I feel like most women would kill for a husband who wants to communicate more with them. I feel like most women would love a husband who wants to pay for someone to do the yardwork.

But no. I have a wife who refuses to tell me if fried chicken is okay without bread. And why? Because she's shopping at a Target with Amanda? I mean, maybe if you're at Walmart you've got an argument. Walmart is the best store on the planet. But Target isn't even open twenty-four hours a day. No wonder she's in a hurry!

All right. I guess I better order. If I wait any longer on lunch it's gonna be dinner.

Oh. That reminds me.

[*Ring . . . Ring . . . Ring . . . Ring*]

LAURA: Yes?

NATE: We're having pizza for dinner tonight, right? That's what we decided yesterday?

LAURA: Well, I decided today to do grilled chicken salads for dinner. No bread, white or wheat.

NATE: Today!? You can't re-decide today something we already decided yesterday! Pizza is fun! I was ready to have something fun tonight! Grilled chicken salads aren't fun! And how am I supposed to have chicken twice in one day? It's a dry, un-fun meat! That seems like very relevant information you should've shared with me before I ordered my lunch.

LAURA: Have you ordered yet?

NATE: No! But that's not the point! The point is I'm back at square one!

LAURA: Have ham! Have beef! Nate, I'm getting in the checkout line—

NATE: What about after dinner?

LAURA: What do you mean "after dinner"?

NATE: Well, I want to know what your plans are. Because I was very set on watching a Jason Statham movie by myself on the family room sofa.

LAURA: By yourself? Again? Nate, it's the *family* room. It's meant for the whole *family*. Besides, you watched Jason Statham movies every night for the last week!

NATE: I love his movies. They're just fun. He's got a wide variety of not variety. What did you wanna watch?

LAURA: One of my *Housewives* shows, I don't know.

NATE: No—no, I'm sorry. I have to put my foot down.

LAURA: Oh, so you're putting your foot down on my *Housewives*?

NATE: Yes. I need at least a day's advance notice about a change in my schedule that big. It's like talking to a kid about when you're going to leave the house. You gotta ease them into things. You can't go, "We're heading out the door! Right now!" just out of the blue and expect things to go smooth. You gotta build up to it.

LAURA: Even a kid doesn't need a whole day! You give a kid, like, ten minutes!

NATE: I am a very sensitive kid.

LAURA: You won't let this go, will you?

NATE: Do I ever?

LAURA: You get Jason Statham alone tonight. But I get grilled chicken salads for dinner, and tomorrow night we're watching *Housewives* in the family room.

NATE: How come you get two things and I only get one?

LAURA: Sorry, I'm at the register! Don't want to be rude to the cashier! Bye!

NATE: Bye.

[*Click*]

Is a day's notice so wrong? I've been planning on watching Jason Statham for at least two days now. Maybe more! Frankly, it doesn't matter how many times I have already watched it. The only thing that matters is that I had my whole night laid out. I was gonna finish working later. On something. Then we were going to eat pizza, which we decided on yesterday and which is fun. And then I was going to watch Jason Statham by myself on the sofa.

This is what I had planned for, and this is what I have been mentally preparing for since at least last night, when I basically did the same thing. If Laura wants to lay out on the couch too—well, that just throws everything off. And *Housewives*? Why does she even want to be around me for that show? That's a chick show!

I know I have a chick brain, but that is definitely a way I do *not* have a chick brain. Laura's dude brain should love watching Jason Statham over and over. It's the nature of dude!

All right. I guess I should order lunch now.

Umm. Huh.

What was I gonna get again? Golly!

[*Ring . . . Ring . . . Ring . . .*]

LAURA: Hello.

NATE: Hey.

[*Silence*]

LAURA: Yes? Is everything okay?

NATE: Yeah.

LAURA: Okay then. See you at home?

NATE: Yes.

[*Click*]

Whatever.

I'll just order a burger and fries. Take *that*, grilled-chicken-salad-tonight.

THE BARGATZE WAY

My parents just decided to move into a little condo. Because when you're old I guess it seems like a good idea to cram the million things you own into an even tinier space.

If you have ever moved, you know that movers are not something you should skimp on when it comes to money. These are basically random strangers you are hiring to put their random-stranger hands all over your stuff. Stuff that can break. Stuff that you eat. Stuff that you wear. It's actually kind of gross when you think about it. So I try not to think too much.

But my mom and dad do not like to spend money, especially on things that make sense. So I told them I would pay for the movers. I didn't just offer. I begged them. I pleaded with them. I said, "Please, let me hire someone good for you. I swear you will regret it if you do not."

My mom just said, "Nathan, we can't. It's the Bargatze Way."

Oh. All right then. If you put it like that.

So my parents went out, and they found themselves a couple dudes to handle the entire move. To this day, it is unclear where they found these men. My parents have no memory of the event. They may have been guys from church. Maybe from an ad in the paper. Maybe they just showed up at the house one day for something completely different, like to fix the water heater, and my folks said, "Hey, wanna give us a hand?" No one knows, but whoever they were, moving was definitely not their full-time job.

I mean, these guys didn't even own their own truck. They rented one. For the day. So when 5 p.m. rolled around and they weren't even close to finishing the job, they said, "Sorry. But getting to U-Haul is our number one priority. If you want, we can come back tomorrow with a hatchback and a ball of twine."

The very last thing they moved was my parents' fridge. The dudes hauled it out of the house and immediately started dragging it across the front yard, flat on its back. Which is literally the one thing you cannot do when you're moving a fridge.

My dad was like, "Hey fellas, I think you're not supposed to do that."

They said, "What do you know?"

My dad goes, "Well, it says so in the fridge manual. And on Google. And on the back of the fridge. Something about the fluids moving around . . . "

They go, "Who's the moving professional here?"

When my parents got to their new, much smaller home, they plugged in the refrigerator, and it wouldn't get cold. The repairman came out the next day, took one look at the banged-up back of the refrigerator, and said, "What kind of idiot puts a fridge flat on its back?"

My dad said, "A professional one."

It was a brand-new fridge. Brand-new. And my folks had to buy another brand-new fridge to replace it, all because they tried to save a few bucks on the movers. Later on, me and my wife Laura came by to see their new place. And to bring some of the stuff the "professionals" didn't have time to move.

"That fridge must've cost ten times more than decent movers," I said. "So you're so cheap, you ended up spending *more money*. It makes no sense!"

My mom sighed and said, "It's the Bargatze Way."

I mean, I get where it comes from. We were so poor when I was growing up. So poor.

Our house was so little that my parents used the den as their bedroom. Then, when they got tired of sleeping there, they switched to the dining room. Then they'd switch back to the den. It was the closest thing we had to moving to a new house.

When my parents bought the place, the Realtor was like, "It has a view of Old Hickory Lake and everything!" And yeah, if you got onto our roof, stood on your tiptoes, and then went to a better roof, you could see this sliver of blue from the lake about a mile away, right by where all the big rich-people houses were. Which were definitely not our house.

But even the way we lived poor didn't make much sense. Here my parents were, saving every penny they could by sleeping on the kitchen table, which actually counted as a third move after the den and the dining room. For us, going out somewhere special to eat meant McDonald's, and even then there was a "water only" rule for our drinks. This is why I now have a "Diet Coke only" rule for every meal of the day.

So what did my mom and dad do? They went out and bought themselves a big fancy car. It was a Chevrolet. And they knew it was fancy because it had cup holders. To my parents, cup holders were something only rich-people cars had.

For years, they'd driven tiny Fords or cheap little Toyotas. Shoddy automobiles without a single proper place to put your drink. And what happened? They'd spilled their beverages everywhere, that's what happened. They'd burned their hands on their mugs of coffee. They'd stained their cheap plastic upholstery every time they'd splurged on Big Red, my dad's favorite soda, which was big and red, and its stains did not come out of anything.

"Why should the poor suffer like this?" they thought. "Don't our cups also deserve to be cradled by their very own holders, inexpensive though our drinks may be? We refuse to live like this!"

Even now, if me or my brother or sister buys a car, the first thing my parents ask is, "Does it have cup holders?" As long as we say yes, they say, "We did right by you kids." And if they're retractable, my dad will be like, "You overpaid."

So my parents went crazy and bought the big Chevy with the cup holders. And it was a bad, bad idea. They were constantly behind on their payments, which were a whopping $100 a month. My mom even had to call her poor sister—literally, she was also poor—for help. My aunt Judy was my godmother, and I imagine my mom saying something like, "Don't you want your godson to have a decent place to put his

The cup holder car. You can tell how fancy it was.

sippy cup on the way to daycare? *Don't you?*" It helped that Aunt Judy was Catholic, so guilt worked on her really good.

Now, I ask you—wouldn't it have been more logical for my parents to get rid of the car so they could afford, I don't know, a bedroom? Why didn't we all just take the bus? I wish I could give you an answer. I do. But I don't got one.

If you ask my mom and dad, they just say that when we were poor they did dumb stuff. But to this day, they still do dumb stuff. If I'm being honest, being logical with money was never the Bargatze Way.

When I got to be an adult—or at least something that kinda resembled an adult—I thought, "Finally, I get to make my own rules. I'm gonna spend as much money as I want. It's about to get crazy around here."

Except I was a comedian, so I didn't have money. At best I got paid free drinks at the bar, as long as those drinks were "water only." And then I started going out with Laura, and she turned out to be even weirder about money than my family. If I'm being honest, I think half the reason my folks liked her was because they couldn't believe how gosh darn cheap she was.

Laura's kind of cheap is a whole different wrinkle to the Bargatze Way. Like the lawn chairs that are currently behind our house. For a long time, they did not exist. Our lawn was chair-less. It was sad. Why? Because for over a year, my wife could not decide which ones to buy.

She got seven estimates on seven kinds of chairs. She did a bunch of research on everything you can think of—on materials, on manufacturing, reading customer reviews. Everything. Then there was planning around the sales—maybe she should wait for Presidents' Day? Or the Fourth of July? When could she get the best possible deal on these chairs?

To Laura, she was making the most intelligent purchase on a long-term investment in lawn furniture. To me, she was basically insane. At the end of the entire process, she calculated—she, not me—that she saved a grand total of eighty bucks. Eighty. Bucks. Well, that's neat.

But what about the cost of all those empty, chair-less days? What about the price of all those hours we spent not being able to sit in our own backyard? A yard that went completely un-sat in! Can those non-chair minutes ever be bought back? No. I don't think so.

I've said before that Laura's so responsible that being with her is like being with my dad, but actually it's more like having a boss.

Back when we lived in New York and I was just getting started, she was the only one who was making any real money. At one point she'd thought about getting into the music business, but by now she was nothing but practical. She interviewed at some big business place, and she told the interviewer, "My husband has a dream. I don't have a dream, so we're going to do his." And her future boss went, "You're hired!" So Laura controlled all our finances—our credit cards, our checking account, everything. Every month, she would look at our shared credit card bill, and she'd say, "What is this charge at Macy's? Why did you spend all this money at Lids? How many hats does one man need? We're living on a budget here, you know!"

It was like a company card, if you worked for the least fun company in the universe.

It got so bad that I actually had to ask my parents, who obviously hated spending money, to start secretly putting money in an old account I had. This was a joint account my mom had set up for me at the bank where she worked. They'd deposit a little money for me every now and then. Just fifty bucks here and there. It was our secret. My own little slush fund. Thank God Laura never found out.*

But even that situation wasn't great. My dad had two or three magician friends in New York, and he'd have these guys ride by our place

---

*Hey, this is Laura. Of course I knew about the slush fund. The Bargatzes are horrible at keeping secrets. Oh, and please don't tell Nate I busted into his computer to write this. He thinks no one knows the password is OldBlue626#, after his car, but we all know. It's the only password he uses for everything.

and check on me. Make sure I really was working at the comedy clubs every single night, and not just spending that $50 on, I don't know, life. I'd be going inside the Boston Comedy Club on Third Street, and I'd see some weird dude in a black cape and a top hat with a red carnation lurking by the corner, and he'd say in this mysterious voice, "Manage your savings wisely!" and he'd just vanish. Then I'd go to a bodega and buy some donuts.

So it felt like I was basically working three full-time jobs at once. I had one gig writing up detailed spending reports for my wife about how many hats I decided to buy at the mall this weekend, or why I chose to pay for a cab instead of just taking the subway last Tuesday. I had another gig meeting with various magician-accountants to prove I was working very hard for the $50 a month my parents gave me. And on the side sometimes I did comedy.

One time I wanted to go on vacation with Laura. No big deal, just take a quick break from my three demanding careers like I was a normal person. Just a normal human being who went on vacation. So I thought it might be nice to go to San Francisco. Maybe we could see Alcatraz or something. But still. I needed money.

So I called my parents and said, "This isn't just a vacation. I'm doing research for work."

They were like, "Research?"

"Yeah. I'm gonna write jokes about Alcatraz. You know, funny prison stuff."

There was a pause. "All right, we'll put a hundred bucks in your account."

I didn't see any magicians following us on the Golden Gate Bridge. But I'm still trying to figure out how to work my bit about sharpened toothbrush shivs into my act.

When me and Laura got married, it wasn't only love and romance. It was like a business merger between my parents and my wife. The weirdest people in the universe when it came to money. It was like we created a monster of bargain-basement prices.

Our engagement was actually pretty cool, but that's because I was in charge of it. We were in New York for that, and I surprised Laura with this hansom cab I rented, like with the horses. It took us around for the afternoon and dropped us off at this nice restaurant at the Central Park Boathouse. And I had the ring and I got champagne and I got down on one knee to propose and everything.

Of course, my parents paid for lunch. And the ring. I sent them the bill and said, "This ain't for work. Hope it's okay." But I picked out the ring myself and everything, and Laura still doesn't know.*

But the wedding? That was planned by my mom and Laura, and it was a whole other story. We had it at a country club in Old Hickory, which I guess sounds pretty nice—until you realize we held it on Friday the 13th. The unluckiest day of the year. (And also, as you may recall, the day before a big Vandy football game.) So the club basically said, "We will pay *you* money to get married on this date, because everyone else will be home hoping they don't get murdered by a dude in a hockey mask."

And even then my dad was like, "Hey, I'll do a few free magic shows for y'all for a discount. If we survive the axe murderer."

The photographer was a buddy of ours who happened to own a camera. Or maybe it was disposable. I can't remember. For all the group shots, he'd go, "How 'bout y'all stand here in the dead sun. Yeah. With the light right in your eyes. That looks real pretty." So in all our pictures we've got these big squints on our faces, almost like we're confused, as in, "Why did we hire this man again?" We saved a few bucks, but the damage to our retinas was priceless.

Most famous, though, was the one-legged DJ. I did mention him in one of my specials, but it bears repeating: We had a one-legged DJ. His

---

*Laura here again. Obviously I knew about this too. Now that I think about it, go ahead and tell Nate. I can't wait to see the look on his face.

lack of both a leg and any understanding of music makes sense when you understand that he was not an actual DJ but an old customer at the bank where my mom worked. She basically said, "This man has bounced a check twice over the last year, and his credit is in the toilet. But how hard can it be to play a record?"

He showed up wearing a T-shirt, put that record down—that one record—told us it was Billy Joel's "White Wedding," and then he played it for the rest of the night. Over and over and over.

Later, me and my buddy P-P went into the bathroom to do his namesake, and we found the DJ sitting there on the countertop with his leg propped up on the urinal—I can't remember if it was the fake leg or not—pulling a packet of cigarettes out of his sock, and lighting up for a smoke. We go, "What is this, Vietnam?"

He coughed and spat and growled, "Bud, I could tell you some stories." Then he put on a hockey mask, and we ran for our lives.

Anyway. Lovely ceremony. Only spent $3,000 on the whole thing. (And if you can't remember how P-P got his name at this point—I mean, even *I'm* not that bad at reading.)

After we got married, I still had the slush fund account through my parents. I mean, of course I did. I was still making barely any money.

Then one weekend me and my comic buddy Dustin went to Vegas. And yes, I know how bad that sounds. If anything, I wish it *was* as bad as it sounds. Because it was actually pretty dull. Unlike Alcatraz, I really was there for work. So there weren't any slot machines. There wasn't any booze. I didn't even eat at any buffets, which is too bad, because to me that's what Vegas is all about.

Everyone else is like, "Party! Whatever happens in Vegas stays in Vegas! *Wooo!*" And I'm like "Lukewarm food under heat lamps! All you can eat! I'll take a doggie bag! *Weeeee!*"

But no. I didn't even do that. We just hung out in our room. But this was back when you needed a phone line to connect to the internet, and we were online all the time, so when we checked out it looked like we'd used our hotel phone all day every day. The bill was $500, which for us might as well be a million bucks.

My friend also didn't have any money, and I was the only one who had a bank, so I wrote a check on my old account. It got overdrafted, so I had to call my parents to help me out, and it became a whole thing.*

My dad says, "Vegas! You used our money to *gamble*?"

I go, "No, this time really was for work, I swear."

He's like, "Oh yeah? I'm still waiting on those Alcatraz jokes."

I'm like, "And you will be waiting a very long while."

Anyway, that was the end of the slush fund. The funny thing is, we were in Vegas, so the place was swarming with magicians. There were twenty of them hanging out at our hotel alone. Would it have been that hard for my dad to have five or six of them check up on us? Maybe give us a little advice on not using your hotel phone for internet?

Honestly, he only had himself to blame.

Years later, I was finally doing good enough to get a house of our own back in Tennessee. Nothing crazy. Just a house.

And I made a decision. I had enough of the Bargatze Way. If we needed to get our porch fixed, I didn't want to get twenty estimates for a porch. I didn't want to spend five years researching the best kind of porch while we sat there with a broken porch. I didn't want to go to church and ask around to see if someone's cousin's best friend's neighbor who was actually a plumber also happened to know something about fixing porches. Bonus points if he knew that Billy Idol and not Billy Joel sang "White Wedding."

If we needed our porch fixed, I just wanted to call up 1-800-PORCH and get it done. I wanted to hire Mr. Porch to come out to my house to

---

* Still Laura here. This one I actually did not know about. But it checks out.

build me the best porch anyone had ever seen. I didn't need to be rich. I just wanted to be not insane.

This is a lot to ask of my family.

One of the first things I promised to do was never mow the lawn, ever again. I spent basically every day of my childhood mowing our lawn. I don't know if the grass in Old Hickory grows faster than the grass of other towns. But I do know that my parents only gave birth to me so they'd never have to pay anyone to mow it for them. They had my brother and sister to help perform other manual labor. Washing windows, vacuuming the rug, selling matchbooks to help pay off all those fancy cup holders. That kind of thing.

So when we moved into the house the first thing I did was tell Laura that we were never gonna mow the lawn ever again. I was gonna pay someone to do it for us.

"Why?" she said. "The grass gets long, so you mow it. How hard is that?"

"But I had to mow the grass all the time as a little kid."

"Yeah," she said. "My guess is grass got long back then too."

But I finally got her to agree to let me hire a service. And I didn't ask anyone from church. I didn't walk down the street hitting up random strangers with slightly green thumbs. I didn't even open up the phone book. I just picked up my phone, dialed 1-800-MR-LAWN and whoever it was who answered, that's who I hired. Didn't even ask the price. All good by me.

I got very excited as the day for our first visit from the lawn service got closer. Looking back, though, I should've figured out something was off. One afternoon, Laura pressure-washed and sealed our entire driveway. To this day, I don't even know what that means. Sealed it from what? It's concrete! You put concrete on top of stuff to *seal that other stuff*! It makes no sense!

Laura had also been talking about getting a security system. And one day I came home and found my sister Abigail dangling out of a second-story window, drilling a hole through our brick wall—that's right, *drilling a hole through our brick wall*—to wire a little camera outside. I know even less about brick than I do about concrete, but I do know my sister shouldn't be drilling holes literally through our house. At least Laura would know how to seal it, I guess.

For all that, though, I still had my lawn service coming at the end of the week. I knew I could count on Mr. Grass, or whatever. He was a true professional. And nothing would take that away.

I drove up that afternoon, and there was the dude—the dude I was paying a reasonable, totally sane amount of money to—wearing a hat and some earmuffs and riding the mower across our lawn. He turned around, and obviously it was my wife. The service had been canceled.

"This ain't so bad!" she shouted. "Maybe I'll do it as a side hustle!"

So yeah. Next time you need your lawn mowed, your driveway sealed, your brick drilled, or a refrigerator dragged flat on its back across your front yard, just call 1-800-BARGATZE.

We work real cheap.

CONCLUSION:
CONGRATS

Hey guys. If you've made it all the way through my book—congratulations, you have officially read more books than I have.

If you read it all in one sitting, that actually does not sound all that healthy, if I'm being honest. You should probably move around some more. Or sprinkle in some other healthier activities, like watching TV, or eating gummy bears while watching TV. And if you did not make it all the way through my book, why am I even talking to you? You're not even here right now.

This book actually took me two years to write. I know. A little longer than I planned, by maybe two years, give or take. Turns out it is not easy to create something so incredibly simple. It took me one year just to finish the chapters with all the blank pages. The copyediting on those was brutal.

But now that I'm done, I feel pretty good about this whole process. The world of books is in the same place as it was before I entered it, which was basically my goal. Who knows—for my next project, I might be even more ambitious. Maybe try Russian historical fiction or dystopian sci-fi. I'm just kidding. I don't even know what any of that means. It's really up to my daughter Harper, anyway, because she's the one who does the real work.

Thanks. We'll keep you posted.

ACKNOWLEDGMENTS

It's been an amazing couple years, you guys. I mean, I've been working as a comic for over twenty years now, and I've enjoyed every minute of my journey, even the early days when I was just getting started. Maybe especially those. Then suddenly, for reasons I still can't exactly figure out, everything went crazy. But in a really, really good way. I'm talking specials, I'm talking *SNL*, I'm talking TV shows and movies in development, the podcast, the touring, this book—it's all gone nuts.

And I just want to say I'm so incredibly grateful to everyone out there for everything. I'm grateful to my family, to my friends, and to all the entertainment types who've been willing to take a chance on me. I'm grateful to the people of Nashville and to everyone out there who's stood by me and had my back. And most of all I'm grateful to God. I truly believe this life can't be about me. It is about Him.

So if your name isn't listed below, just know that I love and thank every single one of you. And please blame the copyeditor, not me. But I would like to shout-out a few people who especially helped with the making of this book.

First off, a big shout-out to Old Hickory, my hometown.

Next, thank you to Laura and Harper. You're the reason I do everything I do. At least all the good stuff.

To my family. Especially my mom, my dad, my brother, and my sister. Thank you not only for being with me and supporting me on this whole incredible journey but thank you specifically for all your help on this book. You guys remembered a ton of great stuff and so many details that really helped bring all these stories to life.

To all my friends, especially P and Michael Clay. I feel so blessed to still be close to people I've known since forever. You guys helped make this a better book, and I'm grateful for it. Thanks for all the convos. And a special thanks to Trey Pearson for helping put me and Michael Clay together in the first place.

Shout-out to my barber-trainer Eric Miller. I promise we'll work out tomorrow.

To Jerry Seinfeld. There's nothing more mind-blowing than the chance to work with my hero. Thank you.

To my managers, Alex Murray and Tim Sarkes. Thank you for helping me navigate all this amazing craziness.

To Suzanne O'Neill, Morgan Spehar, and the entire team at Grand Central Publishing. Thank you for believing in this book, for guiding it, and for helping it make at least a little sense.

To Albert Lee, Christy Fletcher, and the entire UTA team. Thank you for your faith and for keeping this project on track.

To Chris Farah. I guess we finally figured it out. Would not have or could not have done this without you.

To the community at Village Well. Thank you for all the support and encouragement.

To Cyndi, Travis, Abigail, and the entire Nateland Team. Thank you for making all of this possible with all your hard work.

To every single one of my fans. I literally wouldn't be able to do this without you. Thank you so much for believing in me. It might not always seem like it, but I do have a plan and I hope you keep rolling with me.

ABOUT THE AUTHOR

Nate Bargatze is a Grammy-nominated comedian, podcaster, actor, director, and producer from Old Hickory, Tennessee. Hailed as "The Nicest Man in Stand-Up" by *The Atlantic*, Nate is well-known for his specials, including *The Tennessee Kid*, *The Greatest Average American*, *Hello World*, and *Your Friend, Nate Bargatze*. Nate is one of the top-selling touring acts, breaking venue attendance records with more than 1.2 million tickets sold on his Be Funny tour. Nate also runs Nateland Entertainment, a family-friendly content company where he produces stand-up comedy specials, showcases, sketches, and scripted episodic content for film, television, podcasts, music, and more. He lives in Nashville with his wife and daughter.

ABOUT THE AUTHOR

Nate Bargatze is a Grammy-nominated comedian, podcaster, actor, director, and producer from Old Hickory, Tennessee. Hailed as "The Nicest Man in Stand-Up" by *The Atlantic*, Nate is well-known for his specials, including *The Tennessee Kid*, *The Greatest Average American*, *Hello World*, and *Your Friend, Nate Bargatze*. Nate is one of the top-selling touring acts, breaking venue attendance records with more than 1.2 million tickets sold on his Be Funny tour. Nate also runs Nateland Entertainment, a family-friendly content company where he produces stand-up comedy specials, showcases, sketches, and scripted episodic content for film, television, podcasts, music, and more. He lives in Nashville with his wife and daughter.